GEOGRAPHERS'
A-Z VISITORS' LONDON
ATLAS and GUIDE

CONTENTS

© 1996 Copyright by the Publishers
GEOGRAPHERS' A-Z MAP COMPANY LTD.
Fairfield Road, Boroug
Telephone: 01732 781

Showrooms: 44 Gray's
London WC2X 8HX
Telephone: 0171-242-

An A to Z Publi

Edition 22 1996
Printed in Great Britain by BPC Hazell Books Ltd

D0981432

PLACES OF INTEREST, MUSEUMS and ART GALLERIES

Note 1. Each place name is followed by the reference to its map position; e.g.**Admiralty** Whitehall is to be found in square 4A on page 74.

(Places preceded by an * asterisk are outside Central London area mapped.)

Note 2. Each station name is followed by the reference/s (abbreviated) to the Underground Line/s and/or Main Railway Region/s serving it. For example, **Goodge St.** N means that station is on the Underground Northern Line.

Abbreviations are:

(a) UNDERGROUND LINES: B=Bakerloo; Cen.=Central; Cir.=Circle; D.=District; H.=Hammersmith & City; J.=Jubilee; M.=Metropolitan; N.=Northern; P.=Piccadilly; V.=Victoria.

See Underground Map, back cover.

(b) MAIN LINE RAILWAY REGIONS: ER.=Eastern; LMR.=London Midland; SR.=Southern; WR.=Western.

Admiralty, Whitehall. 4A 74
Once the administrative and operational centre of the British Navy, it has become the headquarters of the Home Civil Service. The old building dates from 1722, the handsome screen by Adam being added in 1760. There are valuable paintings and furniture in Admiralty House.
Station: Charing Cross B.J.N.

Admiralty Arch, Trafalgar Square. 3A 74
This large triple archway opens on to the Mall and the quiet of St. James's Park. State and Royal processions pass through it on their way between Buckingham Palace and Westminster Abbey and/or the Houses of Parliament.
Station: Charing Cross B.J.N.

Albert Memorial, Kensington Gardens. 1E 81
Designed by Sir Gilbert Scott, it was erected as a memorial to Prince Albert, Consort of Queen Victoria, at a cost of £120,000, and took 20 years to construct.
Station: South Kensington Cir.D.P.

Alexander Fleming Museum, St Mary's Hosp., Praed St. 4A 58
The laboratory in which Fleming discovered penicillin, displays and video presentation. Open: 10 a.m. to 1 p.m. Mon. to Thurs. and other times by appt. *Station:* Paddington B.Cir.D.H.

Apsley House, Hyde Park Corner. 5A 72
This Adam's building was bought by the famous Duke of Wellington as his London House. It is now the Wellington Museum and contains trophies of the Napoleonic Wars, uniforms, swords and decorations.
Admission Charge. Open: Tues to Sun., 11 a.m. to 5 p.m.;

Closed: Mon., Christmas Eve and Day and Boxing Day.
Station: Hyde Park Corner P.

Bank of England, Threadneedle Street.   5F 65
In the seven-storied Bank, rebuilt on its island site of some
three acres, many old features are reproduced and Soane's
old external wall is preserved. Incorporated under Royal
Charter in 1694 to find for the Government £1,200,000
required for the war against France's Louis XIV.
Station: Bank Cen.N.

Bank of England Museum, Bartholomew La.   4F 65
The history of the Bank of England from its foundation in
1694 to its role today as the nation's central bank. Displays
include banknotes, coins, gold bullion, interactive videos
and a reconstructed 18th century banking hall. Open: Mon.
to Fri. 10 a.m. to 5 p.m. Closed Sat. and Sun. *Station:* Bank
Cen.N.

Bankside Gallery, Hopton Street.   2B 76
Gallery of the Royal Society of Painters in Water-Colours
and Royal Society of Painter-Etchers and Engravers. Open
during exhibitions 10 a.m. to 8 p.m. Tues. 10 a.m. to 5 p.m.
Wed. to Fri. 1 p.m. to 5 p.m. Sunday. Closed Monday.
Station: Blackfriars.

Banqueting House, Whitehall.   4B 74
Commissioned by James I, and built by Inigo Jones, it was
completed in 1622; and embellished by Charles I, with the
famous painted ceiling by Rubens. The artist was rewarded
with £3,000 and a knighthood. It was through a window
of the Banqueting House that King Charles went to his
execution in 1649. It is the only surviving building of
Whitehall Palace. *Admission Charge.* Open: 10 a.m. to 5
p.m. Closed: Sun. *Station:* Charing Cross B.J.N., Westminster Cir.D.

Barbican.   2E 65
A large area of post-war redevelopment designed to rein-
troduce a balanced residential and cultural life back into the
heart of the business City. Pedestrians are segregated from
traffic on elevated levels, and accommodation is grouped
around squares, gardens and lakes. The historic church of
St. Giles and a length of the Roman and Medieval City
Wall are incorporated. The precinct includes the following:
Barbican Centre for Arts and Conferences, Museum of
London, Guildhall School of Music and Drama, City of Lon-
don School for Girls. Opened in 1982 the Barbican Arts
Centre is the London equivalent of the Lincoln Center,
New York or the Centre Pompidou, Paris; facilities include:
Barbican Hall, Barbican Theatre, The Pit (studio theatre),
Barbican Library, Art Gallery, Cinemas, conference and
trade exhibition space, roof-top Conservatory, restaurants
and car park.
Station: Barbican Cir.M.H.

Battle of Britain Museum. See Royal Air Force Museum.

Belfast, H.M.S., Symon's Wharf, Morgan's Lane.   3C 78
This 10,500 ton cruiser, launched in 1938, the last major warship of the 1939–45 war still afloat, is now a naval museum. A ferry service runs from Tower Pier.
Admission Charge. Open: Summer 10 a.m. to 5.30 p.m., Winter 10 a.m. to 4.00 p.m. Closed Christmas Eve and Day, Boxing Day, New Year.
Station: London Bridge N.SR.

*Bethnal Green Museum of Childhood, Cambridge Heath Rd., E2. This branch of the Victoria and Albert Museum has outstanding collections of toys, games, dolls and doll's houses; also children's costume; many activities for children. The local history collection includes displays of Spitalfields silk. Open: weekdays 10 a.m. to 5.30 p.m. Sun. 2.30 to 5.30 p.m. Closed Fridays, Good Fri., Christmas Eve and Day and Boxing Day.
Station: Bethnal Green Cen., Cambridge Heath ER.

Big Ben. Westminster.   1C 74
The name of the $13\frac{1}{2}$ ton bell which strikes the hours in the clock tower of the Houses of Parliament. It was cast at the Whitechapel Foundry in 1858. The tower stands 320 feet. *Station:* Westminster. Cir.D.

Billingsgate, Lower Thames Street.   2A 78
The name of London's oldest market, it was restricted in the 17th century to dealing in fish. The 1874 Market Hall façade is incorporated into the redeveloped site following the removal of trading to the Isle of Dogs in 1982.
Station: Monument Cir.D., Tower Hill Cir.D.

Bomber Command Museum. See Royal Air Force Museum.

Bond Street.   1C 72
The upper end which runs into Oxford Street is New Bond Street, and the lower end which runs into Piccadilly is Old Bond Street. This expensive London shopping street ranks in world fame with the Rue de la Paix in Paris, and New York's Fifth Avenue.
Station: Bond Street Cen.J., Green Park J.P.V.

Bow Street.   5C 62
Is famous for its former Police Court (associated with the "Bow Street Runners"); also as the home of the Royal Opera House. *Station:* Covent Garden P.

Bramah Tea & Coffee Museum, Maguire St.   SE1 5E 79
Shows the history of the tea and coffee trade; including a collection of over 1000 tea pots and coffee makers. *Admission Charge.* Open: daily 10 a.m. to 6 p.m. *Station:* London Bridge N. Tower Hill Cir.D.

British Library, Great Russell Street.   3B 62. In the pro-

cess of moving to new premises   3A 54. Created in 1973 it contains the former library departments of the British Museum and shares the same building. There are several exhibition rooms housing many items of great historical interest including Magna Carta, Lindisfarne Gospels, Nelson's Log Books.
Open: 10 a.m. to 5 p.m. Sun. 2.30 p.m. to 6 p.m.
READING ROOM (ticket holders). Among notable people who have studied here are Thackeray and Karl Marx.
Open: 9 a.m. to 5 p.m. (9 p.m. Tues., Wed., Thurs.) Closed Sun., Good Friday, Christmas Eve and Day, Boxing Day, New Year's Day and the week beginning the first Monday in May.
Station: Russell Square, P., Tottenham Court Road Cen.N.

British Museum, Great Russell Street.   3A 62
Originally founded in 1753 from several private collections, it rapidly became the finest Museum in existence. Its unrivalled collections are comprised in the Departments of Coins and Medals, Egyptian Antiquities, Western Asiatic Antiquities, Greek and Roman Antiquities, (including the famous Elgin Marbles), British and Medieval Antiquities, Oriental Antiquities. See also Natural History Museum and Museum of Mankind.
Open: weekdays 10 a.m. to 5 p.m.; Sun. 2.30 to 6 p.m.
Closed: Christmas Eve and Day, Boxing Day and Good Friday, New Year's Day. Free lectures on certain days.
Station: Russell Square P., Tottenham Court Road C.N.

Broadcasting House, Portland Place.   3C 60
This building, the headquarters of B.B.C. Sound, was completed in 1932. Audiences are sometimes invited to listen to broadcast performances in the Concert Hall.
Station: Oxford Circus B.Cen.V.

Buckingham Palace.   1C 84
London Palace of Her Majesty Queen Elizabeth II. When she is in residence the Royal Standard flies from the mast. Changing of the Guard takes place daily at 11.30 a.m. (alternate days in winter months). Built by the Duke of Buckingham in 1703. Buckingham Palace was bought by George III in 1761, was rebuilt again by George IV, and became Queen Victoria's London home. Refaced in 1913. The Queen's Gallery, which forms part of the private chapel destroyed in the Second World War, contains a varying exhibition of masterpieces and works of art from the royal art treasures. Open: During August and September, for details see Telephone Guide page 48. Ticket office in St James's Park. *Admission Charge.*
QUEEN'S GALLERY *Admission Charge.* Open: March to January daily 9.30 a.m. to 4 p.m.
ROYAL MEWS *Admission Charge.* Open: 12 to 4 p.m.

Wed. only Jan. to March. Tues. Wed. & Thurs. March to early Aug. Mon. Tues. Wed. & Thurs. Aug. & Sept. *Station:* Green Park J.P.V., St. James's Park Cir.D., Victoria Cir.D.V.

Bunhill Fields, City Road.   1F 65
For two centuries until 1852 the chief Nonconformist Burial Ground, John Bunyan, Daniel Defoe, William Blake and John Wesley's mother are among the famous people buried here. Milton wrote 'Paradise Lost' in Bunhill Row and died there. John Wesley was buried in Wesley's Chapel opposite, and George Fox was buried in the adjoining Quaker burial ground.
Station: Old Street N.

Cabinet War Rooms, Clive Steps, King Charles St., SW1.   5A 74
One of the Second World War bunkers used by Winston Churchill and his staffs. On display are the Cabinet Office, Central Map Room, Churchill's Office and bedroom, the Transatlantic Telephone Room; all restored to their war time appearance.
Admission Charge. Open: 10 a.m. to 6 p.m. daily.
Station: Westminster.

*Camden Passage, N1
A popular centre for antique arcades and shops.*Station:* Angel N.

*Carlyle's House, 24 Cheyne Row, SW3
The famous writer lived here from 1834 until his death in 1881. The house has hardly been altered since. Now a National Trust property.
Admission Charge. Open: April to October 11 a.m. to 5 p.m. Wed. to Sun. Closed Mon. and Tues.; and November to March.
Station: Sloane Square Cir.D.

Carnaby Street.   5D 61
Popular Teenage Fashion Centre of the late 1960's.
Station: Oxford circus B. Cen. V., Piccadilly Circus B.P.

Cenotaph, The, Whitehall.   5B 74
Designed by Sir Edwin Lutyens, it now stands as a perpetual memorial to 'The Glorious Dead' of both World Wars. On the Sunday nearest November 11th of each year, crowds gather at the Cenotaph for the two minutes' silence, and wreaths are laid by the Queen, members of the Government and other mourners.
Station: Charing Cross B.J.N., Westminster Cir.D.

Central Criminal Court, Old Bailey.   4B 64
Known as 'The Old Bailey', the present building was completed in 1907 on the site of Newgate Prison. The lofty tower is surmounted by a bronze gilt figure of Justice. During important trials in Court 1, a large crowd gathers

outside the Old Bailey in the hope of gaining admission to the Public Gallery, in Newgate Street, which seats 28. Five other courts seat up to 32 each. Open: 10.15 a.m. until the rising of the Courts. *Station:* St. Paul's Cen.

Central Hall, Tothill Street.   1A 86
This large domed building is the Methodists' London Headquarters. It is often used for conferences, exhibitions and concerts. The first session of the General Assembly of the United Nations took place here in 1946.
Station: Westminster Cir.D., St. James's Park Cir.D.

*Chelsea Physic Garden, 66 Royal Hospital Rd., SW3
Botanic gardens est. 1673 for the propagation and study of new species; several staple industries in former British colonies were derived therefrom.
Admission Charge. Open: Easter to Oct. Suns and Wed. 2–5 p.m. Entrance in Swan Walk.

Cheshire Cheese, The Old, Wine Office Court, 145 Fleet Street.   4A 64
An old and little-altered inn, famous for its Pudding, served at lunch times between Oct. and April. Tradition has it that Dr. Johnson, Boswell and Oliver Goldsmith were *habitués*. Built in 1667 over cellars dating back to 1538. Open: Bar daily Mon. to Sat. Restaurant Lunch daily, Dinner Mon. to Sat. 071-353 6170.
Station: Blackfriars Cir.D. & SR.

*Chiswick House, Burlington Lane, W4
A fine example of Palladian architecture built by Richard Boyle the Third Earl of Burlington in the late 1720's. The main front is composed of two double approach stairways flanking a classical portico at first floor level. The interior with its series of connected rooms was designed by William Kent. There are marble fireplaces with support panels by Sebastian Ricci and paintings by Kneller, Lely and Guido Reni. The garden laid out by Kent was a forerunner to the English Landscape Park and contains some statues brought over from Hadrian's Villa at Tivoli near Rome. There are also statues of Palladio and Inigo Jones. *Admission Charge.* Open: 10 a.m. to 6 p.m. summer months; to 4 p.m. winter months. *Station:* Chiswick from Waterloo SR.

Christie's, 8 King Street.   3E 73
Is greatly reputed for its Auction Sales of valuable paintings, furniture, silver, jewels, etc. held regularly. Telephone 0171 839 9060 for details.
Station: Green Park J.P.V.

Clarence House, St. James's Palace.   5E 73
The London residence of the Queen Mother.
Station: Green Park J.P.V.

Cleopatra's Needle, Victoria Embankment.   3D 75
An Egyptian obelisk which, about 3,500 years ago, stood

in front of the Temple of the Sun at Heliopolis. When it was being towed to England in 1877, this 'Needle', $68\frac{1}{2}$ feet high and weighing 180 tons, had to be abandoned in the Bay of Biscay during a storm. Its sister column is sited in Central Park, New York. *Station:* Embankment B.Cir.D.N.

Clink Exhibition, The Clink Prison, 1 Clink St., SE1   3F 77
Illustrates the infamous low life of this area, once known as "The Liberty of the Clink". *Admission Charge.* Open: daily 10 a.m. to 6 p.m. *Station:* London Bridge N.

Clore Gallery, see Tate Gallery.

College of Arms, or Heralds College, Queen Victoria Street. 1C76 Deals with all matters relating to Heraldry, genealogy and State Ceremonials and consists of three Kings of Arms (Garter, Clarenceux, and Norroy & Ulster), six Heralds and four Pursuivants, appointed by the Sovereign. The building, Derby House, reconstructed after the Great Fire, was presented to the College by Queen Mary I (Mary Tudor) in 1554. The panelled Earl Marshal's Court is open 10 a.m. to 4 p.m. Mon. to Fri. (also open for heraldic enquiries). See also Heralds Museum in Tower of London. *Station:* Blackfriars Cir.D. & SR., Mansion House Cir.D.

*Commonwealth Institute, Kensington High Street, W8
A centre for information about the Commonwealth in one of London's most spectacular modern buildings. Built with money and gifts of materials contributed by the Commonwealth, it contains permanent exhibition galleries, an art gallery, a cinema and a reference library. There are also lectures, conferences and other extramural educational activities. Open Mon. to Sat. 10 a.m. to 5 p.m.; Sun. 2.00 to 5 p.m. Closed Christmas Eve and Day, Boxing Day and Good Friday. Events include films, music, dance, drama, etc. *Station:* Kensington High Street Cir.D.

County Hall, Westminster Bridge.   5D 75
Situated on the south bank of the Thames; once the Headquarters of the London County Council; also of the Greater London Council (G.L.C.) disbanded 1986. The main building overlooking the river was opened by King George V in 1922. *Station:* Waterloo B.N., Westminster Cir.D.

Court Dress Collection, see Kensington Palace.

Courtland Institute Galleries, Somerset House, Strand.   1D 75 Contains collections belonging to the University of London, and includes the Courtauld Collection of Impressionist and Post-Impressionist paintings: masterpieces by Manet, Renoir, Van Gogh and Cezanne. *Admission Charge.* Open: 10 a.m. to 6 p.m.; 2 to 6 p.m. Sun. Closed Dec 24, 25, 26, Jan 1. *Station:* Temple Cir.D., Charing Cross N.B.Cir.D.

Covent Garden, Southampton Street, WC2.   1C 66
Originally 'Covent Garden' the square is now ped-

estrianised with the central market hall restored and open as an environment of shops, studios, cafés, promenades and landscaped areas. The Flower Market now houses the London Transport Museum and Theatre Museum. The market given Royal Charter in 1671 grew into London's largest wholesale fruit, vegetable and flower market and has moved to a new site off Nine Elms Lane.
Station: Covent Garden P.

Craft Gallery, 44a Pentonville Rd., N1   2F 55
Crafts Council showcase for artist-craftsmen, changing exhibitions throughout the year. Craftsman Index. Slide Library. Research facilities. Open 11 a.m. to 6 p.m. Tues. to Sat. 2 p.m. to 6 p.m. Sun. *Station:* Angel.

Crafts Centre, Contemporary Applied Arts, 43 Earlham St.   5B 62
Federation of British Craft Societies. Varied exhibitions of work by artist-craftsmen. Open 10 a.m. to 5.30 p.m. Mon. to Fri. 11 a.m. to 5 p.m. Sat. *Station:* Tottenham Ct. Rd.

*Crosby Hall, Cheyne Walk, SW3
15th-century Hall originally part of Crosby Place, a mansion on Bishopsgate, moved to this site in 1910. Oak Hammerbeam roof with oriel window. Open: 10.15 a.m. to 12.15 p.m., 2.15 p.m. to 5 p.m., Sunday 2.15 p.m. to 5.15 p.m. *Station:* Sloane Square Cir.D.

Custom House, Lower Thames Street.   2B 78
Until 1940, the headquarters of the Commissioners of Customs and Excise. This has been the approximate site of successive Custom Houses from the 14th century. The Commissioners are now at Kings Beam House, Mark Lane, EC2. *Station:* Monument Cir.D. Tower Hill Cir.D.

Cutty Sark, see Greenwich page 37.

Design Museum, Shad Thames   5E 79
Covers the history, practice, theory and future of design in mass-produced consumer products and services. *Admission Charge.* Open: 11.30 a.m. to 6 p.m. Mon. to Fri. 12.00 to 6 p.m. Sat & Sun. *Station:* London Bridge N. Tower Hill Cir.D.

Dickens House, 48 Doughty Street.   1E 63
Although the author lived here only from 1837 to 1839, 'Oliver Twist' and 'Nicholas Nickelby' were written and the 'Pickwick Papers' completed during those two years. The house is now a Museum of Dickens Memorabilia, and the headquarters of the Dickens Fellowship.
Admission Charge. Open: 10 a.m. to 5 p.m. Closed Sundays and Bank Holidays. *Station:* Russell Square P.

Dirty Dick's, 202 Bishopsgate.   3C 66
The present tavern, supposed to be part of the old house concerned, owes its name to an 18th-century tragedy.

Nathaniel Bentley, a wealthy dandy, heard of the death of his bride-to-be on the day they were to celebrate their engagement. From then on he took no care of his appearance or of his house, and became known as 'Dirty Dick'.
Station: Liverpool Street Cen.Cir.M.E.R.

Docklands Light Railway, passenger enquiries 0171 222 1234. A spectacular ride from Bank Station IA78 or Tower Gateway ID79 over Docklands; from Tower Gateway only Sat. & Sun. (pedestrian tunnel from Island Gardens links to Greenwich).

Doctor Johnson's House, 17 Gough Square.   4A 64
The famous 18th-century character immortalised by Boswell, lived here from 1748 to 1759. The house contains an early edition of his Dictionary which was compiled here and published in 1755 selling for four guineas. Here also he wrote 'The Rambler' which appeared twice weekly for two years with a circulation of about five hundred.
Admission Charge. Open: Weekdays 11 a.m. to 5.30 p.m. (Oct. to April 5 p.m.). Closed Sundays and Bank Holidays.
Station: Blackfriars Cir.D. & SR.

Downing Street, Whitehall.   5B 74
No. 10 Downing Street is world-famous as the home of the British Prime Minister and the scene of Cabinet meetings. No. 11 houses the Chancellor of the Exchequer, and No. 12 is the Government Whip's office.
Station: Westminster Cir.D.

Duke of York's Column, Waterloo Place.   4F 73
This column, which stands above the steps leading to St. James's Park, is 124 feet high, and was erected in 1833 as a memorial to Frederick, Duke of York, the second son of George III. Although an able and devoted Army administrator as Commander-in-Chief, he was less successful in the field: according to popular song he 'led his ten thousand men up a hill and down again'.
Station: Piccadilly Circus B.P., Charing Cross B.J.N.

*Dulwich College Picture Gallery, College Road, SE21.
An outstanding collection of Flemish, Italian and Dutch Art. Paintings by Ruisdael, Van de Velde, Cuyp, Van Dyck, Rembrandt, Rubens, Claude, Raphael, Veronese, Murillo and Poussin; it also contains British 17th- and 18th- century portraiture, including Gainsborough and Reynolds.
Admission Charge. Open: Tues. to Fri. 10 a.m. to 1 p.m. and 2 p.m. to 5 p.m. Sat. 11 a.m. to 5 p.m. Sun. 2 to 5 p.m. Closed Mon., Christmas Eve and Day, Boxing Day, New Year's Day and Good Friday.
Station: North Dulwich from London Bridge N. & SR., West Dulwich from Victoria Cir.D.V. & SR.

*Earl's Court, Warwick Road, SW5
Large exhibition halls for national events and other shows.

The Royal Tournament is held here annually.
Station: Earls Court D.P., West Kensington D.

Ely Place.   3A 64
The site of Ely Palace, London home of the Bishops of Ely in which John of Gaunt died in 1399. Demolished in 1772 it is now a private cul-de-sac of 18th-century houses still watched over by a beadle at the gated entrance. The only remains are Ely Chapel or St. Etheldreda's Church the first pre-Reformation Church to be restored to Roman Catholic worship. *Station:* Farringdon Cir.M.

Eros, see Piccadilly Circus.

Faraday Museum, Royal Institution, 20 Albermarle St.   2D 73 Devoted to Michael Faraday's work and life including his own laboratory and equipment. Admission charge. Open 1 p.m. to 4 p.m. Mon. to Fri.
Station: Green Park.

Fleet Street.   2D 73
Traditionally, but no longer the centre of the British newspaper industry, following the introduction of modern technology in new premises mainly in redeveloped dockland sites. *Station:* Temple Cir.D., Blackfriars Cir.D. & SR.

Florence Nightingale Museum, Lambeth Palace Road,   1D 78
Illustrates the life and work of this famous woman, including a life size recreated ward at the Crimea.
Admission Charge. Open: 10 a.m. to 4 p.m. Tues to Sun.
Station: Westminster Cir.D. Waterloo B.N.

*Geffrye Museum, Kingsland Road, E2.
Housed in Almshouses erected in 1715 by the Ironmongers' Company, it comprises a series of period rooms dating from the 16th to the 20th century, containing furniture, domestic equipment and musical instruments from middle class homes.
Open: 10 a.m. to 5 p.m.; Sun. 2 to 5 p.m. Closed Mondays, except Bank Holidays. *Station:* Old Street N.

Geological Museum, see Natural History Museum

Goldsmiths' Hall, Foster Lane.   4D 65
Home of the Goldsmiths' Company, one of the twelve Great Livery Companies of the City of London. Since 1281 a jury containing several goldsmiths has been responsible for the Trial of the Pyx, the testing of newly minted coins, and from 1870 this has been held annually at Goldsmiths' Hall. Gold and silver are assayed and hallmarked here, but the Assay Office is not open to the public. The Company possesses one of the most representative collections of antique plate in the country, a notable example being the coronation cup of Queen Elizabeth I. In recent years an

11

impressive collection of modern silver and jewellery has been built up here.

Admission: By ticket. Enquire at City Information Centre.
Station: St. Paul's Cen.

Gray's Inn, High Holborn.   2E 63
One of the four great Inns of Court, entered through an archway on the north side of High Holborn. The historic Elizabethan Hall has been fully restored since the war. The Chapel also suffered damage by bombing. Francis Bacon, who was a student of the Inn, is said to have planted the catalpa tree in the gardens.
Station: Chancery Lane Cen. (closed Sundays).

Green Park.   4C 72
Covers an area of 53 acres. The fine iron gateway on the Piccadilly side is that of old Devonshire House.
Station: Green Park J.P.V., Hyde Park Corner P.

Greenwich, see page 37.

Guard's Chapel, see Guards Museum.

Guards Museum, Birdcage Walk   1E 85
Illustrates the 300-year history of the Brigade of Guards. Adjacent is Guard's Chapel, rebuilt 1963 incorporating surviving apse of the earlier chapel devastated 1944 by a flying bomb during a morning service with the loss of 121 lives.
Admission Charge. Open 10 a.m. to 4 p.m. Closed Fri.
Station: St James's Park.

Guildhall, Gresham Street.   4F 65
Has been the centre of civic government in the City of London for more than a thousand years. It dates from 1411–39. The original building, except the porch, the crypt with its lovely vaulting, and the structure of the Hall, was destroyed in the Great Fire of 1666. The Great Hall is used for the Presentation of the Freedom of the City and other civic functions. Here the Livery Companies, twelve of whose banners hang from the walls, annually elect the new Lord Mayor and Sheriffs. The Lord Mayor's procession is held on the second Saturday in November and the banquet the following Monday.
Open: Mon. to Sat. 10 a.m. to 5 p.m.; Sundays Summer only and Spring and Summer Bank Holidays. A modern extension adjoining contains the important Guildhall Library (Reference only) and the Corporation of London Record Office—regarded as the most complete collection of ancient municipal records in existence. Open 9 a.m. to 5 p.m. Mon. to Sat. Closed Sun. The Library also houses the Clockmaker's Company Museum—illustrating 500 years of timekeeping.
Station: Bank Cen.N. & SR.

Guinness World of Records, Trocadero Centre, Piccadilly Circus.   1F 73

An exhibition designed to transform the 'Book of Records' into an exciting three-dimensional presentation. Admission charge. Open 10 a.m. to 10 p.m. daily. Closed Xmas Day.
Station: Piccadilly Circus

Hampton Court Palace, see page 38.

Hatton Garden, Holborn.   2A 64
Stands partly on the site of the old palace of the Bishop of Ely. It is well known as the important centre of the world's diamond trade.
Station: Chancery Lane Cen. (closed Sundays).

Hayward Gallery, see South Bank Arts Centre page 27.

H.M.S. Belfast. See "Belfast".

Horse Guards, Whitehall.   4B 74
These barracks were rebuilt in 1753. Two mounted guardsmen are on sentry duty here, and the Changing of the Guard daily at 11 a.m., Sundays 10 a.m., is a picturesque sight. Trooping the Colour, a magnificent ceremony, takes place on the Queen's official birthday on the parade ground at the rear of the building.
Station: Embankment B.Cir.D. Charing Cross B.J.N. & SR.

Houses of Parliament, Parliament Square.   1C 86
Stand throughout the world as a symbol of democratic government. Rebuilt in 1840 on the site of the old Palace of Westminster, which was destroyed by fire, this is the largest building erected in England since the Reformation. When Parliament sits, a flag flies from Victoria Tower by day, and by night a light in the Clock Tower burns above the famous Big Ben.
For admission to hear debates apply to an M.P.; or join the public queue for the Stranger's Gallery outside St. Stephen's Entrance. Otherwise open only by arrangement with an M.P.
Station: Westminster Cir.D.

House of Detention, Clerkenwell Close EC1   1A 64
Experience 300 years of crime and punishment in London's underground prison. *Admission Charge.* Open: daily 10 a.m. to 5.15 p.m. *Station:* Farringdon Cir.D.M.

Hyde Park.   3B 70
This Royal Park covers 341 acres. On the south side from Hyde Park Corner westwards, many people take an early morning ride in Rotten Row before going to business. On Sundays the park is crowded, and it is then that the famous 'tub-thumping' public orators on rostrums and soap boxes near Marble Arch air their views to groups of listeners. The Serpentine, a large lake in the centre of the park, provides boating, and is one of London's Lidos (open from the last Saturday in April until the second Sunday in October).

Station: Hyde Park Corner P., Knightsbridge P., Lancaster Gate Cen., Marble Arch Cen.

Imperial War Museum, Lambeth Road. 3A 88
Records and illustrates all aspects of warfare, military and civil, allied and enemy, in which Britain and the Commonwealth have been involved since August 1914. Includes works of art; photographic and film records; and printed and manuscript material. Dramatic recreations with sounds, smells and special effects include WW1 "Trench Experience" and WWII "Blitz Experience". Admission charge.
Open: 10 a.m. to 6 p.m. daily. (Free from 4.30 p.m. daily). Closed Christmas Eve and Day, Boxing Day, Good Friday, New Year's Day. Reference Dept. Mon. to Fri. 10 a.m. to 5 p.m. By appt. Free lectures and films on certain days.
Station: Lambeth North B., Elephant and Castle B.N.

Jewish Museum, 129/131 Albert St. 1C 52
Contains antiquities in silver, wood, ivory, pottery and textiles, illustrating Jewish domestic and public worship.
Open: 10 a.m. to 4 p.m. Sun. to Thurs. Closed Fri. & Sat. Conducted tours of parties can be arranged by prior appointment with the Secretary/Curator.
Station: Mornington Crescent N.

*Keats House, Wentworth Pl., Keats Grove, NW3.
Keats Regency home (1815) between 1818–20. Museum of personal relics.
Open: 10 a.m.–1 p.m., 2–6 p.m.; Sat. 10 a.m.–1 p.m., 2–5 p.m. Sunday 2–5 p.m. (Winter months not Mon. to Fri. a.m.)

Kensington Gardens. 3D 69
Formerly the grounds of Kensington Palace, now a woodland park where children gather at the Round Pond to sail their boats or around the statue of Peter Pan. The Long Water should be seen from the bridge that divides it from the Serpentine.
Station: High Street Kensington Cir.D., Lancaster Gate Cen., Queensway Cen.

Kensington Palace, Kensington Gardens. 4C 68
Designed by Wren for William III, Queen Victoria was born here. The London home of the Prince and Princess of Wales. Two portions are open to the public, the 'State Rooms' and the 'Court Dress Collection'.
Admission Charge. Open: Daily 9 a.m. to 5 p.m., Sun 11 a.m. to 5 p.m. (last admission 4.15). Closed Christmas Eve and Day, Boxing Day, New Year's Day and Good Friday.
Station: High Street Kensington Cir.D., Queensway Cen.

*Kenwood, Hampstead, NW3
A classical style mansion set in 24 acres of parkland once owned by the first Earl of Mansfield. Designed by Robert

Adam 1767–9 with additions by Saunders in 1795. Bequeathed to the Nation by the late Lord Iveagh in 1927, complete with his fine collection of paintings and furniture. Lakeside open air concerts held in the summer.
Admission Charge. Open daily 10 a.m. to 6 p.m. Oct. to March daily 10 a.m. to 4 p.m. Closed Christmas Eve and Day, Good Friday. Park open 8 a.m. to dusk.
Station: Archway N. then Bus.

Kew Gardens, see page 38.

Knightsbridge. 1D 83
Famous area for high quality shopping, especially Harrods on Brompton Road. *Station:* Knightsbridge.

Lambeth Palace, London. 3D 87
Has been for over 700 years the residence of the Archbishop of Canterbury. Of particular interest is the Library with its 1,700 manuscripts.
Open: By appointment only.
Station: Westminster Cir.D., Lambeth North B.

Lancaster House, Stable Yard, London. 4D 73
This early Victorian mansion is known for the splendour of its State Apartments.
Station: Green Park J.P.V., St. James's Park Cir.D.

Leadenhall Market, Leadenhall Street. 5B 66
Victorian glass and Iron hall of 1881. Once specialised in poultry, now in quality delicatessen shops. *Station:* Monument Cir.D.

Leicester Square. 2A 74
Was laid out from 1635–70, and named after the Earl of Leicester, whose residence was on its north side. Hogarth and Joshua Reynolds also lived here.
Station: Leicester Square N.P.

Lincoln's Inn, Chancery Lane. 4D 63
One of the four inns of Court which have the power of 'calling to the Bar'. The Law Library, built in 1845, is the finest in London and contains over 70,000 volumes and many fine MSS. Of particular interest are the early 16th-century gateway to Chancery Lane and the Inigo Jones chapel erected in 1623.
Admission: To the Inn, on application. To the Chapel, free. Sunday service 11.30 a.m., during sittings.
Station: Chancery Lane Cen. (closed Sundays), Holborn (Kingsway) Cen.P.

Lloyd's, Lime Street. 5B 66
This international insurance market and world centre of shipping intelligence is named after Edward Lloyd's coffee house, the 17th-century rendezvous of people interested in shipping. The famous Lutine Bell is rung when an announcement of special importance is to be made from the Rostrum, particularly with regard to overdue vessels.

The exciting modern building has external observation lifts giving public access to the Underwriting Room Viewing Gallery and exhibition on Lloyd's history. Open to pre booked organised groups only 10 a.m. to 2.30. Mon. to Fri. only.
Station: Aldgate Cir.N., Bank Cen.N.S.R., Monument Cir.D.

Lombard Street. 5A 66
Famous as the centre of banking, it owes its name to the Lombard goldsmiths and money-lenders who established themselves here after the expulsion of the Jews in 1290.
Station: Bank Cen.N. & SR.

London Bridge. 3A 78
There have been many bridges on this site, the first having been built by the Romans. The present bridge replaced the 1831 stone bridge, now in Lake Havasu City, Arizona, U.S.A. *Station:* London Bridge N.S.R., Monument Cir.D.

London Bridge City. 4C 78
A traffic-free environment of offices, shops, apartments, restaurants, and leisure facilities, incorporating the Victorian Hay's Dock buildings now "Hay's Galleria", a riverside walk with panoramic views of the 'city' and access to HMS Belfast linking London Bridge and Tower Bridge.
Station: London Bridge.

London Canal Museum, New Wharf Rd IC 54
Tells the story of London's canals, including the role of working horses; housed in what was an industrial ice house, built in the 1850's for Carlo Gatti the ice cream manufacturer. *Admission Charge.* Open: Tues. to Sun. 10 a.m. to 4.30 p.m.
Station: King's Cross, St. Pancras Cir.D.P.N.V.M.H.

London Dungeon, The. Tooley St. 4B 78
An exhibition of gruesome and macabre events from the Dark Ages until the end of the 17th century, not recommended by the management to the nervous or unaccompanied children. *Admission Charge.* Open: 7 days a week 10 a.m. to 5.30 p.m. summer, 10 a.m. to 4.30 p.m. winter.
Station: London Bridge.

London Pavilion, see Piccadilly Circus.

London Planetarium, Marylebone Road. 1F 59
A vast hemispherical dome on which, by a £70,000 Zeiss projector, images of the celestial bodies are shown, accurate in size, brightness and position relative to each other; also their relative paths and speeds through the night sky. *Admission Charge.* Performances regularly 12.20 to 5 p.m. Sun. 10.20 a.m. to 5 p.m. Closed Christmas Day. Tel: 0171-486 1121 for details.
Station: Baker Street B.Cir.J.M.H.

London Stone, Cannon Street. 1F 77
This stone is believed to have been the millarium from which the Romans measured the distances out of the City. It was moved in 1798 to its present position.
Station: Cannon Street Cir.D. (closed Sundays) & SR.

London Telecom Tower, entrance in Maple St. 2D 61
This 620 ft. structure was built to facilitate tele-communications without interference from other tall buildings.
Station: Warren Street N.V., Goodge Street N.

London Toy & Model Museum, 23 Craven Hill, W2. 1E 69. Closed for refurbishment until Spring 1995.
Shows the history and development of commercially made toys and models, featuring period shop displays.
Admission Charge. Open 10 a.m. to 5.30 p.m. Mon. to Sat. Sunday 11 a.m. to 5.30 p.m. *Station:* Lancaster Gate C.

London Transport Museum, Covent Garden. 1C 74
Historic vehicles and exhibits including early steam and electric locomotives, horse-buses, motor buses (including the famous 'B' type), tram cars, trolley buses, posters, tickets, signs, etc. Housed in a magnificent Victorian structure with cast iron arcades and glazed clerestories.
Admission Charge. Open daily 10 a.m. to 6 p.m. Closed Christmas Day and Boxing Day.
Station: Covent Garden P.

London Zoo, Regent's Park. 1F 51
Tel: 0171-722 3333. The 'lure of the wild' in the heart of London; a day among the thousands of animals here is a day with a difference. Special attractions include the aquarium, the walk-through Snowdon Aviary, the Moonlight World where day and night are reversed, the Penguin Pool—an essay in delicate curves, the Elephant House—a great concrete fortress. There's a Childrens Zoo; various rides and animal encounters and animal feeding takes place at certain times. *Admission charges.* Open March to Oct. 10 a.m. to 5.30 p.m. Nov. to Feb. 10 a.m. to 4 p.m.
Station: Camden Town N. Regent's Park B.

Madame Tussaud's, Marylebone Road. 1F 59
World-famous waxwork exhibition where visitors wander among lifelike historical and contemporary figures.
Admission Charge. Open: 10 a.m. to 5.30 p.m. Mon. to Fri. 9.30 a.m. to 5.30 p.m. Sat. & Sun. Closed only on Christmas Day.
Station: Baker Street B.Cir.J.M.H.

Mansion House. 5F 65
This, the first official residence of the Lord Mayors of London, was built in 1753. Until this time the Mayors had to receive in their own homes. The famous banquets given by the Lord Mayor take place in the Egyptian Hall. The Mansion House Justice Room is in the same building.

Admission: Alternate Saturday afternoons only on application by post to The Private Secretary to The Rt. Hon. The Lord Mayor.
Station: Bank Cen.N. & SR.

Marble Arch, Oxford Street.   1E 71
Originally intended as an entrance to Buckingham Palace, this 'triumphal arch' was made too narrow for the State Coach and became a gate into Hyde Park. Later, the park boundary was moved back, leaving Marble Arch an entrance to nowhere. Nearby, where Edgware Road intersects Bayswater Road, stood Tyburn Gallows, where public executions took place until 1783.
Station: Marble Arch Cen.

Marlborough House, Pall Mall.   4F 73
Built by Wren in 1709 for the great Duke of Marlborough, it reverted to the Crown in 1817. Amongst its occupants have been Edward VII when Prince of Wales, and George V until his accession. From 1911 until her death it was the residence of Queen Alexandra. Queen Mary lived here when in London. Now a Commonwealth Conference Centre. Adjoining the house is QUEEN'S CHAPEL 1627, designed by Inigo Jones. Services: Sun 8.30 and 11.15 a.m. Easter Day—end of July.
Station: Green Park J.P.V.

Middlesex Guildhall, Broad Sanctuary.   1A 86
The former County Hall built by J. S. Gibson 1905–13, it stands on the site of the old belfry of Westminster Abbey.
Station: Westminster Cir.D.

Monument, The.   1A 78
A fluted Doric column erected by Sir Christopher Wren in the year 1677 to commemorate the Great Fire of London of 1666. Its height is 202 feet, which is the distance to the house in Pudding Lane where the fire broke out. The view from the top repays the climb of 311 steps.
Admission Charge. Open 31st March to 30th Sept. Mon. to Fri. 9 a.m. to 6 p.m. Sat. & Sun. 2 to 6 p.m. Other months Mon. to Sat. 9 a.m. to 4 p.m. Closed Sun. the public being admitted until 20 minutes before closing. Closed Good Friday, Christmas Day and Boxing Day.
Station: Monument Cir.D.

Museum of Childhood, see Bethnal Green.

Museum of Garden History, Lambeth Palace Road.   3D 87. Formed by the Tradescant Trust in the restored St. Mary-at-Lambeth church in honour of the Tradescants—gardeners to Charles I, and responsible for the introduction of many exotic plants into England. Voluntary contributions appreciated. Open 11 a.m. to 3 p.m. Sun. 10.30 a.m. to 5 p.m. March to December. Closed Sat.
Station: Westminster

Museum of London, London Wall. 3D 65
One of London's modern, purpose-built museums: constructed as part of the Barbican it is designed to lead visitor's through the chronological development of London and environs from prehistoric times to the present day. Imaginative displays and excellent facilities earned it Museum of the Year award 1978. *Admission Charge.*
Open: Tues. to Sat. 10 a.m. to 6 p.m. Sun. 12.00 to 6 p.m. Closed Mondays, also Christmas and Boxing Day. Free lectures on certain days.
Station: Barbican Cir.M.H. (closed Sun.) St. Paul's Cen.

Museum of Mankind, Burlington Gardens. 2D 73
Ethnography Department of the British Museum. Exhibitions portraying the lives and cultures of peoples throughout the world.
Open: 10 a.m. to 5 p.m. Mon. to Sat. 2.30 p.m. to 6 p.m. Sun. Closed Christmas Eve and Day, Boxing Day and Good Friday.
Station: Piccadilly Circus P.

Museum of Methodism, see Wesley's House.

Museum of the Moving Image, South Bank. 3E 75
Devoted to the history and development of cinema, television and video, including displays on pre cinema and future technologies; also changing exhibitions.
Admission Charge. Open: 10 a.m. to 6 p.m. daily. Closed Christmas. *Station:* Waterloo.

*National Army Museum, Royal Hospital Road, Chelsea. Museum of the British Army, of the Indian Army to 1947, also colonial and auxiliary forces.
Open: 10 a.m. to 5.30 p.m. daily. Closed Good Friday, Christmas Eve and Day, Boxing Day and New Year's Day.
Station: Sloane Square Cir.D.

National Gallery, Trafalgar Square. 2A 74
One of the most important picture galleries in the world, containing a collection representative of every European school of painting and works by nearly all the Great Masters. The Gallery was opened in 1824 with the Angerstein Collection of 38 pictures.
Open: 10 a.m. to 6 p.m.; Sundays 2 to 6 p.m.; Closed Christmas Eve and Day, Boxing Day and Good Friday. Free lectures on certain days.
Station: Embankment N., Charing Cross B.J.N.

National Maritime Museum, see Greenwich page 37.

National Portrait Gallery, St. Martin's Place. 2A 74
National collection of portraits of famous British men and women dating mainly from the Tudor dynasty to the twentieth century.

Open: 10 a.m. to 5 p.m., Saturdays to 6 p.m., Sundays 2 to 6 p.m. Closed Good Friday, Christmas and Boxing Day. *Station:* Leicester Square N.P., Charing Cross B.J.N.

National Postal Museum, King Edward St.   2C 64
Philatelic collections, drawings, documents & library.
Open: 9.30 a.m. to 4.30 p.m., Mon. to Fri. Closed Sat. & Sun. *Station:* St. Paul's Cen.

National Theatre, see South Bank Arts Centre page 28.

National Westminster Tower, Old Broad St.   4B 66
600 feet high, it incorporates three irregular shaped wings around a central core.
Station: Liverpool Street C.D.H.

Natural History Museum, Cromwell Road.   3F 81
One of the world's finest collections of natural history and earth sciences (including the galleries of the former Geological Museum). As well as the traditional displays e.g. Zoology, Entomology, Palaeontology, rocks, minerals and fossils (including moon rock), the museum features new stimulating visual learn-and-enjoy style exhibitions including Hall of Human Biology, Man's Place in Evolution, Introducing Ecology, Dinosaurs and Their Living Relatives, Origin of Species, British Natural History, Story of the Earth, Britain before Man. The Children's Centre can provide trail sheets for an indoor nature trail.
Admission Charge. Open: 10 a.m. to 5.50 p.m.; Sun. 11.00 a.m. to 5.50 p.m. Free lectures on certain days. Closed Christmas Eve and Day, Boxing Day and Good Friday.

New Scotland Yard, Broadway.   2F 85
The Headquarters of the Metropolitan Police and of its Criminal Investigation Department. Formerly situated on Victoria Embankment.
Admission: To visiting police officers only.
Station: St. James's Park Cir. D.

*Olympia, Hammersmith Road, W14.
It covers an area of ten and three-quarter acres, and is one of the most famous showplaces and exhibition centres in the world.
Station: Kensington (Olympia) D. (Exhibitions only.)

Operating Theatre Museum, 9a St. Thomas' St.   4F 77
An original Victorian operating theatre, with instruments, apparatus and Herb Garret. Open: 10 a.m. to 4 p.m., Tues to Sun. Admission charge.
Station: London Bridge N.

Oratory, The, Brompton Road.   3B 82
Built in the Italian Renaissance style during the 19th century, it is well known for its fine musical services. Cardinal Newman served here as priest after his conversion from the Anglican to the Roman Catholic faith.
Open: 7 a.m. to 8 p.m. daily.

Station: South Kensington Cir. D.P.

Oxford Street. 5B 60
A principal shopping street. Remarkably straight for London, it is on the site of the old Roman road leading west from the city.
Station: Bond Street Cen.J., Marble Arch Cen., Oxford Circus B. Cen.V., Tottenham Court Road Cen.N.

'Petticoat Lane', Middlesex Street. 3D 67
A street market for a numerous variety of goods, where, on Sunday mornings, bargain-hunters and passers-by are attracted to the stalls of persuasive salesmen.
Station: Aldgate East D.M., Liverpool Street Cen.Cir.M.E.R.

Photographers Gallery 5 Gt. Newport St. Off Charing Cross Rd 1A 74
Changing exhibitions by living photographers and pictures from the past; bookshop and print sales.
Open 11 a.m. to 7 p.m. Tues to Sat.
Station: Leicester Square.

Piccadilly Circus. 2F 73
A swirl of people, traffic and coloured lights; this traditional focal point of London is emerging from much needed modernisation; including the creation of a pedestrian piazza linking the famous Eros statue to the South Side. Both the Trocadero Centre and the London Pavilion provide traffic-free environments of shopping and leisure facilities—see the Rock Circus, London Experience and Guinness World of Records.
Station: Piccadilly Circus B.P.

Pollocks Toy Museum, 1 Scala Street. 3E 61
Of particular interest to children. Toy theatres, games, dolls, dolls' houses and toys, etc.
Admission Charge. Open: 10 a.m. to 5 p.m. Mon. to Sat. Closed Sun.; Christmas and Boxing Days and Easter Mon.
Station: Goodge Street N.

*Portobello Road Market, W11.
A lively general market with much dealing in antiques, Victoriana, pseudo-antiques.
Station: Ladbroke Grove or Westbourne Park M.

Post Office Tower, see London Telecom Tower.

Public Record Office, Chancery Lane. 4F 63
Store-house for public archives, documents, State papers and National records, with public search rooms for research and study. Open: Mon. to Fri. 9.30 a.m. to 5 p.m., last call for documents at 3.30 p.m.; readers tickets on application to the Secretary. (More modern documents and facilities at Ruskin Avenue, Kew) MUSEUM of historical items including the Domesday Book, signatures and documents relating to many important people, Nelson, Wellington, Shakespeare etc.

Open: Mon. to Fri. 10 a.m. to 4.45 p.m. Closed Bank Holidays.
Station: Chancery Lane Cen. (closed Sundays), Temple Cir.D. (closed Sundays).

Queen's Gallery, see Buckingham Palace page 5

Queen's Tower, off Exhibition Road.   4F 81
287 ft clock tower, all that remains of the Imperial Institute. 324 steps lead to a viewing gallery with an unrivalled panorama over London.
Admission Charge. Open: 10 a.m. to 5.30 p.m. July, Aug. Sept. *Station:* South Kensington.

Queen Victoria Memorial, The Mall.   5D 73
Stands in front of Buckingham Palace. Of white marble, the centre figure of the Queen is 13 ft high. Groups on the remaining sides represent Justice, Truth and Motherhood, while the whole is surmounted by a winged Victory.
Station: St. James's Park Cir.D. Victoria Cir.D.V. & SR, Green Park J.P.V.

Regent's Park,   2E 51
One of the largest London parks, it covers an area of 472 acres and contains the Zoo and a large boating lake. Queen Mary's Gardens are famous for roses and open-air plays. The elegant terraces surrounding the Park by John Nash are now well contrasted by two modern buildings, the Royal College of Physicians and the London Mosque.
Station: Baker Street B.Cir.J.M., Regent's Park B.

Regent Street.   1D 73
This important shopping street was first designed by Nash in 1813. Links the West End with Regent's Park.
Station: Oxford Circus B.Cen.V., Piccadilly Circus B.P.

Rock Circus, London Pavilion, Piccadilly Circus.   2F 73
An exhibition and audio-visual experience presenting the story of rock and pop music from the 1950's onwards; features both the stars and their music. *Admission Charge.* Open daily 11 a.m. to 9 p.m. Sun. to Thurs. from 12 noon on Tues. Fri. and Sat. 11 a.m. to 10 p.m. Closed Christmas Day.

Roman Bath, Strand.   1E 75
Brick bath of uncertain origin, 15 feet 6 inches long, fed by a spring. Now a National Trust property.
Not open, but the interior is visible from the pathway.
Station: Temple Cir.D.

Roosevelt Memorial, Grosvenor Square.   1A 72
Britain's personal memorial to President Franklin D. Roosevelt after the Second World War. 160,000 contributions of five shillings each closed the subscription list in less than 6 days. *Station:* Bond Street Cen.J.

Royal Academy of Arts, Burlington House, Piccadilly.   2E

73 Founded by George III in 1768, the first President being Sir Joshua Reynolds. The Annual Exhibition of works by living artists is opened in the main galleries early in May for a period of 12 weeks. The Private View is the first event of the London 'Season'. Gallery Shop and Framing Service. *Admission charges vary.* Open: 10 a.m. to 6 p.m. daily. *Station:* Piccadilly Circus B.P., Green Park J.P.V.

*Royal Air Force Museum, Aerodrome Road, NW9. Portrays the history of aviation, aircraft from World War 1 onwards, uniforms, photographs, etc.
Battle of Britain Hall with its collection of fighter planes, vividly displays the events and those involved in the battle for supremacy of the sky in 1940. Bomber Command Hall tells the story of the development of aerial bombing and displays many famous aircraft.
Open: 10 a.m. to 6 p.m. daily. Closed Christmas Eve and Day, Boxing Day, Good Friday, New Year's Day, and May Day. *Admission Charge.*
Station: Colindale N.

Royal Albert Hall, Kensington Gore.   1F 81
This largest Concert Hall in London, seating approximately 8,000 was completed in 1871.
Station: South Kensington Cir. D.P.

Royal College of Music, Prince Consort Road.   2F 81
Contains the Donaldson Musical Instrument collection of rare instruments, with specimens of most of the early keyboard, stringed and wind instruments. Here also is the acclaimed Britten Opera Theatre opened 1987.
Open: Mon. and Wed 11 a.m. to 4.30 p.m. in term time. Parties by appointment with the Curator only.
Station: South Kensington Cir.D.P.

Royal College of Surgeons, Lincoln's Inn Fields, WC2.   4E 63 Is the headquarters of surgery in England. Teaching, research and examinations are major functions of the College, which contains within its medical museum the Hunter Collection.
Open to members of the medical profession and to others on application to the Secretary or either of the Conservators. *Station:* Holborn (Kingsway) Cen.P.

Royal Courts of Justice, Strand, WC2.   5E 63
These buildings were opened in 1882, enlarged in 1911 and extended in 1968 and 1971. There are 50 Courts, and though the public may enter the body of a Court to hear a case, provided there is room, the proper place is in the Public Galleries. Courts generally sit in Term times: Weekdays, 10.30 a.m. to 4.30 p.m.
Station: Temple Cir.D., Aldwych P. (Rush Hours only).

Royal Exchange, Cornhill.   5A 66
Was opened by Queen Victoria in 1844, replacing two pre-

vious buildings on this site, burned down respectively in 1666 and 1838. The original Exchange of 1568 was modelled on the Antwerp Bourse.
Station: Bank Cen.N. & SR.

Royal Festival Hall, see South Banks Arts Centre.

Royal Geographical Society, Kensington Gore. 1F 81
Founded in 1830, Lowther Lodge designed by Norman Shaw 1874. Important cartographic archives available for public viewing in the map room.
Open: 10 a.m. to 5 p.m. Mon. to Fri. Closed Good Fri. and Christmas. Library by appointment.
Station: Knightsbridge P.

*Royal Hospital, Chelsea, Royal Hospital Road, SW3.
Was designed by Sir Christopher Wren and founded in 1682 by Charles II as a home for old soldiers. The 'Chelsea Pensioner' is a well-known figure in his scarlet (Summer) or dark blue (Winter) coat. The statue of Charles II in the Figure Court is by Grinling Gibbons. In part of the spacious gardens the Flower Show is held annually by the Royal Horticultural Society.
Open: (a) Buildings and Museum open 10 to 12, 2 to 4 p.m. Sun 2 to 4 p.m. Closed Bank Hols. (b) The grounds are open from 10 a.m. to dusk. Sun. and Good Fri. 2 p.m. to dusk, closed Christmas Day. Guide available by previous arrangement.
Station: Sloane Square Cir.D.

Royal Mews, see Buckingham Palace page 5.

*Royal Mint, Tower Hill, EC3   2E 79
It was here that our 'silver' and bronze coins were struck between 1811 and 1970, work since transferred to Llantrisant, South Wales. Prior to 1811 it formed part of the Tower of London. *Station:* Tower Hill Cir.D.

Royal Naval College, see Greenwich page 37.

St. Bartholomew's Hospital, Smithfield.   3C 64
Popularly known as 'Bart's', this is the oldest hospital in London, having been founded in 1123 by Rahere, together with an Augustine Priory, in the reign of Henry I. The building contains portraits of famous physicians and surgeons of the hospital by Reynolds, Lawrence, etc., and Hogarth's 'The Good Samaritan' and 'Pool of Bethesda'. *Admission:* On application to the Clerk to the Governors. *Station:* St. Paul's Cen.

St. James's Palace.   4E 73
Built in 1532 by Henry VIII on the site of a leper hospital, this Palace was from time to time used as a Royal Residence after the Palace of Whitehall had been burned down in 1698. Charles II, James II, Mary II, and George IV were born here, and it was from here that Charles I took leave

of his children before his execution outside Whitehall's Banqueting House. It was also the residence of the Duke of Windsor while Prince of Wales. The main gateway, the Tapestry and Armoury Rooms and the Chapel Royal are all that remain of the original building.

Admission: To the Chapel for the Sunday morning service at 11.15 (Oct.-July).

Station: Green Park J.P.V., St. James's Park Cir.D.

St. James's Park. 5F 73

These 93 acres were acquired by Henry VIII in 1531 to give him hunting near his Palace of Whitehall. It was under Charles II that the land was laid out by the French landscape gardener, Le Notre, to form one of the most charming of London's Royal parks. A variety of water birds inhabit the lake, and these may be identified by labelled reproductions.

Station: St. James's Park Cir.D., Charing Cross B.J.N. SR.

St. Katharine's Dock, St. Katharine-by-the-Tower. 2E 79

Built 1827 to designs by Thomas Telford, since 1968 redeveloped into a mixture of leisure and international trade facilities. New buildings include London World Trade Centre and Tower Hotel. Historic structures have been restored and incorporated. The complex with shopping arcades and cobbled walks centres round the 240 moorings Yacht Haven.

Station: Tower Hill Cir.D.

St. Martin-in-the-Fields, St. Martin's Place. 2B 74

This historic church rebuilt by James Gibbs 1721–61 is a famous Trafalgar Square landmark. Has visitor centre, religious bookshop, craft market, restaurant and Brass Rubbing Centre (see below).

Station: Charing Cross.

St. Paul's Cathedral, Ludgate Hill. 5C 64

This is Sir Christopher Wren's masterpiece, built to replace the much larger Old Cathedral on the same site after its destruction in the Great Fire of 1666. The most prominent of London's buildings, this is an immense Renaissance structure, its exterior length being 515 ft, its width across transepts 250 ft., and the height from pavement to the top of the cross 365 ft. Together with other chapels in St. Paul's there is the American Chapel which was dedicated in the presence of Queen Elizabeth II and the then Vice-President Nixon of the United States. Among the many famous people buried here are Christopher Wren, Nelson, Wellington, Jellicoe, Reynolds and Turner. 627 steps lead to the Galleries and to the Great Ball.

Services held daily. Open for visitors Mon. to Sat. 8.30 a.m. to 4 p.m. Admission charge for sightseers, extra for galleries. Visiting subject to restrictions during services and ceremonies.

Savoy Chapel, Savoy Hill, Strand.   1D 75
The present Chapel was erected as part of a hospital founded under the will of Henry VII. It stands on the site of the old Palace of Savoy given to the Earl of Savoy by Henry III. Chaucer, it is believed, was married here during John of Gaunt's ownership. John of Gaunt had to flee, however, when Wat Tyler's rebels destroyed the buildings in 1381.
Open: Tues. to Fri. 11.30 a.m. to 3.30 p.m. Sun. service 11.00 a.m. Closed August and September.
Station: Aldwych P. (Weekday rush hours only), Embankment N.

Science Museum, Exhibition Road.   3F 81
Renowned and extremely popular collection of scientific, engineering and industrial exhibits both historic and modern. Many of these can be operated by visitors. Special attention is drawn to the Children's Gallery, Aeronautical section, and Wellcome Historical Medical Collection.
Admission Charge. Open: weekdays and public holidays (except Good Friday, Christmas Eve and Day, Boxing Day and New Year's Day) 10 a.m. to 6 p.m.; Sundays 11 a.m. to 6 p.m. Free lectures on certain days.
Station: South Kensington Cir.D.P.

Shakespeare's Globe Theatre & Exhibition, Bankside   3D 77
The reconstructed 1599 Globe Theatre will be the centrepiece of the International Shakespeare Centre. Exhibition and tour open daily 10 a.m. to 5 p.m. Admission charge.
Station: London Bridge N.

Sherlock Holmes Museum, 221b Baker Street.   1E 59
Modelled on the life and times of Sherlock Holmes and Dr Watson as portrayed by Sir Arthur Conan Doyle. Open 9.30 a.m. to 6 p.m. daily. *Admission Charge.*
Station: Baker Street B.Cir.J.M.H.

Silver Vaults, 53 Chancery Lane.   3F 63
Underground strongrooms built in the 1880s as a Safe Depository. Now houses over 40 individual shops selling all types of silverware from contemporary to antique and Sheffield Plate.
Station: Chancery Lane Cen.

Sir John Soane's Museum, Lincoln's Inn Fields.   3E 63
This house, built in 1812 as the residence of Sir John Soane, architect to the Bank of England, contains his own museum, furniture, and library; Egyptian, Greek and Roman antiquities, including the Sarcophagus of Seti 1; paintings by Canaletto, Watteau and Reynolds; and the finest collection of Hogarth's work, comprising the eight scenes of 'The Rake's Progress' and four of 'The Election'.

Open: Tuesday to Saturday, 10 a.m. to 5 p.m. Closed Bank Holidays.
Station: Holborn (Kingsway) Cen.P.

Smithfield. 3C 64
Now chiefly known for its Meat Market. In the past, the 'smooth field' lying outside the city wall was variously used for jousting, for St. Bartholomew's Fair, held annually for centuries, and for many executions. Among those executed here were: William Wallace, beheaded in 1305 for supporting Robert Bruce's claim to the Scottish throne; Roman Catholic and Protestant Martyrs burnt at the stake—during the 16th and early 17th centuries—for their beliefs; Wat Tyler struck dead in 1381 by the Lord Mayor.
Station: Barbican Cir.M., Farringdon Cir.M.

Somerset House, Strand. 1D 75
Was originally the Palace of Edward VI's first Protector, the Duke of Somerset, after whom it is named. At his execution the Palace was forfeited to the Crown. The present building dates from 1775 and houses the Courtauld Institute Galleries (see above), Inland Revenue and the Probate Registry. Famous wills once kept here have been transferred to the Public Record Office. The office of Population Censuses and Surveys has now been moved to St. Catherines Ho., 10 Kingsway WC2. 8.30 a.m. to 4.30 p.m. weekdays. Principal Probate Registry 10 a.m. to 4.30 p.m. weekdays, closed Sats.
Station: Aldwych P. (weekday rush hours only). Temple Cir.D.

Sotheby's, 34/5 New Bond Street. 1C 72
Founded in 1744 it is the oldest and much the largest firm of fine art auctioneers in existence. Sales of furniture, jewellery, silver, porcelain, pictures, books, etc., held regularly except in August. Telephone 0171-493 8080 for details.
Station: Bond Street Cen.J.

South Bank Arts Centre. 3E 75
The variety of public buildings on this, the site of the 1951 Festival of Britain, illustrates the development of British architectural design between the construction of the Royal Festival Hall and National Film Theatre 1951, the Queen Elizabeth Hall, Purcell Room and Hayward Gallery 1967 and finally the National Theatre 1976.
Station: Embankment B.Cir.D., Waterloo B.N. SR.

Southwark Cathedral, London Bridge. 3F 77
This fine Gothic edifice, built upon a nunnery, was originally the church of an Augustinian Priory, founded under Henry I. St. Saviour's was inaugurated as a Cathedral under its present name in 1905. John Harvard, founder of Harvard University, U.S.A., was baptised here in 1607. Exactly 300 years later a chapel and window were erected in his mem-

ory by Harvard students. Fletcher, Massinger and Edmund Shakespeare—brother of William—are buried here. Open daily.
Station: London Bridge N & SR.

Spencer House, 27 St. James's Pl.   7D 73
London's finest surviving 18th century Town House, built 1756–66 for the first Earl Spencer, an ancestor of HRH The Princess of Wales. Open Sundays only 11.30 a.m. to 5 p.m. (closed Aug. and Jan.). Access by guided tour only. *Admission Charge.*
Station: Green Park P.V.

Spitalfields Market, Commercial Street.   2D 67
Home of the former fruit, vegetable and flower market with a fine flower hall. Trading moved to Temple Mills, Waltham Forest in 1991.
Station: Liverpool Street Cen.Cir.M & ER.

Staple Inn, Holborn.   3F 63
Dickens' description in 'Edwin Drood' remains true: 'Behind the most ancient part of Holborn, where certain gabled houses some centuries of age still stand ... is a little nook composed of two irregular quadrangles, called Staple Inn ... the turning into which out of the clashing street imparts to the relieved pedestrian the sensation of having put cotton in his ears, and velvet soles on his boots.' His Mr. Grewgious lived here, and so in real life did Dr. Johnson. Staple Inn, formerly one of the lesser Inns of Court, now houses the Institute of Actuaries.
Station: Chancery Lane Cen. (closed Sundays).

Stock Exchange, The. Old Broad Street.   4A 66
Plays a key part in maintaining London's role as the leading international financial centre, its origins date back to the 16th century when the first joint-stock company was formed.
Station: Bank Cen.N. & SR.

Strand.   2C 74
Universally known for its hotels, theatres and shops. From Trafalgar Square it extends eastwards for nearly a mile.
Station: Charing Cross B.J.N.SR., Aldwych P. (Weekday rush hours only).

*Syon House, London Road, Brentford, Middlesex.
The summer home of the Duke of Northumberland, Syon was originally a monastery built by Henry V in 1415. Much later a new house was built on the site incorporating parts of the monastery. The exterior remains largely unaltered, the interior was redesigned by Robert Adam in the 1760s with typical plasterwork, pillars and statues. There are many paintings, including portraits by Reynolds and Gainsborough. Gardens laid out by Capability Brown.
Admission Charge. Open: HOUSE: Easter to End Sept.

Wed. to Sun. inclusive and Bank Hol. Mondays 11 a.m. to 5 p.m. also Sundays in October. GARDENS: Summer daily 10 a.m. to 6 p.m., Winter 10 a.m. to dusk. Closed Christmas Day and Boxing Day.
Additional attractions include the London Butterfly House, open 10 a.m. to 3.30 daily; *Admission Charge.*
Station: Brentford Central from Waterloo SR.

Tate Gallery, Millbank. 5B 86
The national collection of British painting, modern foreign painting, and modern sculpture. Special collections of Blake, Pre-Raphaelites and Contemporary British School; the modern Clore Gallery extension houses the remarkable Turner Bequest. Special exhibitions of great public interest are announced in the Press. Admission charge to these.
Open: 10 a.m. to 5.50 p.m. Sun. 2 to 5.50 p.m. Closed Good Friday, Christmas Eve and Day, Boxing Day, New Year's Day, May Day.
Station: Pimlico V.

Telecom Technology Showcase, Baynard Ho. Queen Victoria Street. 1C 76 The story of telecommunications; includes working exhibits and video presentations.
Open: 10 a.m. to 5 p.m. Mon. to Fri. Closed Bank & Public Hols.

Temple, Fleet Street. 1F 75
Formerly the property of the Knights Templars—from 1184 to 1313—and then of the Knights of St. John of Jerusalem, it finally came into the possession of two Inns of Court—Inner and Middle.
Open: Middle Temple Hall Mon. to Fri. 10 a.m. to 12 noon, 3 to 4.30 p.m.; Inner Temple Hall Mon. to Fri. 11 a.m. to 12 noon; Temple Church 2 p.m. to 4.30 p.m. daily. All closed for public holidays.
Station: Aldwych P. (rush hours only), Temple Cir.D.

Temple Bar, Strand. 5F 63
Mentioned in records as far back as the 13th century, it was the western entrance gate to the City of London. The last Temple Bar erected by Wren in 1672, is now in Theobold's Park, Cheshunt, Herts. The Griffin Monument opposite the Law Courts marks its original site.
Station: Aldwych P. (Weekday rush hours). Temple Cir.D.

*Thames Barrier, Woolwich Reach.
Built to save London from flooding, the Barrier consists of huge movable steel gates pivoted between concrete piers; hydraulic machinery can lift the gates from the riverbed in 30 minutes. On the south side an exhibition, audio-visual presentation and viewing facilities are open for the public.

Theatre Museum, Russell St., Covent Garden. 1C 74
History of the Theatre from early Elizabethan times to the 1980's including Opera, Ballet, Music Hall, Pop and Pan-

tomime. Also changing exhibitions of theatrical costume, prints; live theatre performances in studio theatre. Admission charge. Open 11 a.m. to 7 p.m. Tues to Sun.
Station: Covent Garden P.

Tobacco Dock, The Highway, Wapping.   2F 79
''London's Shopping Village'', in restored historic dock buildings—quayside setting with sailing ships. Restaurants, car park, open daily. Short walk from Tower of London via East Smithfield E1.
Station: Shadwell, East London line via D.M.

Tower Bridge.   3D 79
Was designed by Barry and Jones and completed in 1894. The opening of the two draw-bridges to allow the passage of large ships is one of the sights of London. A bell rings before the bridge opens, and all traffic has to wait. TOWER BRIDGE WALKWAY (*Admission Charge*) 142 ft. above the Thames. Walkway and historical exhibition open daily 10 a.m. to 4.45 p.m. to 6.30 p.m. Summer months. Closed Dec. 24, 25, 26, Jan 1. Good Fri.
Station: Tower Hill Cir.D.

Tower Hill Pageant, Tower Hill Ter.   2C 78
Discover 2000 years of history, step into a time car and be transported from Roman London through to the Blitz, seeing, hearing and smelling the past. Museum of waterfront archaeological finds. *Admission Charge.* Open daily 9.30 a.m. to 4.30 p.m. (to 5.30 a.m. April to Oct.) *Station:* Tower Hill Cir. D.

Tower of London.   2D 79
Built in part by William the Conqueror in 1078 as a fortress to guard the river approach to London, this is the most perfect example of a medieval castle in England, the outer walls being added later. The White Tower contains, besides its collection of firearms and execution relics, the finest early-Norman chapel in this country. The Crown Jewels are housed in Waterloo Block. Heralds Museum shows history and development of heraldry. Wall Walk gives good views over the Tower and River. Anne Boleyn, Katherine Howard, Lady Jane Grey, Margaret Countess of Salisbury, Jane Viscountess Rochford, Robert Devereux Earl of Essex, were executed on Tower Green.
Admission Charge extra charge for the Jewel House. Open Summer: 9 a.m. to 6 p.m. Mon. to Sat. 10 a.m. to 6 p.m. Sun. June, July, Aug until 6.30 p.m. Winter: 9.30 a.m. to 5 p.m. Mon. to Sat. 10 a.m. to 5.30 p.m. Sun. Closed Good Friday, Christmas Day and Boxing Day, New Year's Day. Jewel House closed all Feb. for cleaning.
Station: Tower Hill Cir.D.

Trafalgar Square.   3A 74
Laid out as a war memorial and named after the victory of Trafalgar, the Square was completed in 1841. In the centre

rises Nelson's Column, 170 ft. high overall, allowing Nelson a view of the sea. The lions at the base are by Landseer. Fountains and pigeons delight onlookers. Facing Whitehall is a 17th-century equestrian statue of Charles I, the Martyr King.

Station: Charing Cross B.J.N. & SR.

Trocadero Centre, see Piccadilly Circus

University of London, Russell Square.   2A 62
This Senate House, completed just before the Second World War, contains only the University Library, Institute of Education, and central administration. Many other Schools and Institutes constituting the University are located nearby; with others throughout the London area, and some beyond.

Station: Russell Square P.

Victoria and Albert Museum, Cromwell Road.   3A 82
One of the great world museums of fine and applied art, it illustrates artistic achievement throughout the centuries and is arranged into two groups. (a) Primary Collections—of style, period or nationality. (b) Departmental Collections—sculpture, textiles, woodwork, etc. The museum incorporates the National Art Library. Open: 12 to 5.50 p.m. Mon. 10 a.m. to 5.50 p.m. Tues. to Sun. Closed Christmas Eve and Day, Boxing Day, New Year's Day, May Day. Crafts shop. Voluntary admission charge.

Station: South Kensington Cir.D.P.

Victoria Embankment.   5C 74
This tree-lined thoroughfare was built in 1864–70 by Sir Joseph Bazalgette, it stretches from Westminster Bridge to Blackfriars Bridge about 1¼ miles and is the shortest and most enjoyable route from Westminster to the City with a variety of things to see. Starting from Westminster Bridge, there is a statue of Boadicea in her chariot by Thomas Thorneycroft 1902, Royal Air Force Memorial, on your left is part of the Victoria Embankment Gardens with the York Watergate in the west corner the only surviving part of York House, the position of the gate indicates the former extent of the river. Beyond the railway bridge is Cleopatra's Needle, Somerset House, Temple and Temple Gardens.

Station: Blackfriars Cir.D. & SR., Embankment B.Cir.D.N., Temple Cir.D., Westminster Cir.D.

Victoria Tower Gardens, Millbank.   2C 86
Views across the river to Lambeth Palace and Church, and downstream to Somerset House and other buildings. Statue of Emmeline Pankhurst, leader of the women's suffrage movement, and a bronze replica erected in 1915 of the Burghers of Calais by Rodin 1895.

Station: Westminster Cir.D.

Wallace   Collection,   Hertford   House,   Manchester Square.   4F 59 The most representative collection in Eng-

31

land of French 18th-century painting, sculpture, furniture and Sèvres porcelain. It includes, as well, masterpieces by Rembrandt, Hals, Rubens, Reynolds, Gainsborough, Van Dyck, Velasquez and Titian; important collections of ceramics, goldsmiths' work, and European and Oriental arms and armour. Formed in the main by the third and fourth Marquesses of Hertford and the latter's son, Sir Richard Wallace. Open: 10 a.m. to 5 p.m.; Sundays 2 to 5 p.m. Closed Good Friday, Christmas Eve, Christmas Day, Boxing Day, New Year's Day, May Day.
Station: Bond Street Cen.J., Baker Street B.Cir.J.M.

Wellcome Centre for Medical Science, 183 Euston Rd.   5F 53
'Science for Life' exhibition aims to explain and celebrate biomedical research, using exciting interactive exhibits. Open: 9.45 a.m. to 5 p.m. Mon. to Fri. 9 a.m. to 1 p.m. Sat.
Station: Euston Square Cir.M.H.

Wellington Arch, Hyde Park Corner.   5A 72
Designed by Decimus Burton in 1828. Originally a statue of Wellington stood on top, this was replaced by the present group when the Arch was moved from the entrance to Hyde Park. The frieze is based on the Elgin Marbles to be seen in the British Museum.
Station: Hyde Park Corner P.

Wellington Museum, Apsley House, Piccadilly.   5A 72
See **Apsley House.**

Wesley's House, Chapel and Museum of Methodism City Road.   1A 66
John Wesley lived here for 12 years and died in this house in 1791. His own rooms and furniture are preserved, and the Museum contains a unique collection of his possessions. Wesley is buried in the graveyard behind the Chapel. The Museum of Methodism is open 10 a.m. to 4 p.m. Mon. to Sat.; closed Bank Hols. *Admission Charge.* Chapel open 8.30 a.m. to 5 p.m. Mon. to Sat. and for Sunday services.
Station: Old Street N., Moorgate Cir.M.N.

Westminster Abbey, Parliament Square.   2B 86
One of the most interesting and historic religious buildings in England; and architecturally one of the masterpieces of the Middle Ages. Founded about 800 A.D., the present edifice was planned and erected as a Royal Mausoleum by Henry III in memory of Edward the Confessor, and until George III, most of the Kings of England were buried within its precincts. Almost all, too, have been crowned here; the only two exceptions being Edward V, who was murdered before he could be crowned, and the Duke of Windsor, Edward VIII, who renounced the throne before his coronation. The famous Coronation Chair is in Edward the Confessor's Chapel. Many famous men are buried in the

Abbey; there is the well-known Poets' Corner, and the grave of the Unknown Warrior. Abbey Museum in the outstanding Norman Undercroft shows the Abbey history and a remarkable collection of Royal and Noble effigies and death masks. Services held daily.
Open: Nave open daily (Sundays between services only). Royal Chapels, Poets' Corner, Choir, and Statesmens' Aisle, Mon. to Sat. only; *Admission Charge*. Chapter House and Museum daily; *Admission Charge*.
Station: Westminster Cir.D., St. James's Park Cir.D.

Westminster Cathedral, Ashley Place.   3E 85
Opened in 1903, this is the foremost Roman Catholic Church in England. The architect, John Francis Bentley, who was influenced by the Christian Byzantine style of St. Sophia at Constantinople, died a year before the building was completed. A lift serves the Campanile, which is 284 ft. high. In May 1982 Pope John Paul II celebrated the first mass ever by a Pope on English soil. Open 7 a.m. to 8 p.m. daily.
Admission Charge for lift to viewing gallery, open usually 10.30 a.m. to dusk, Summer season only.
Station: Victoria Cir.D.V. & SR.

Westminster Hall, Parliament Square.   1B 86
The main surviving fragment of the old Palace of Westminster destroyed by fire in 1834. Erected in 1097 by William Rufus, it was destroyed by Richard II who was responsible for the magnificent oak roof spanning the 68 ft. width of the Hall. Many famous State trials have taken place here; among them those of Charles I, Sir Thomas More, Guy Fawkes and Warren Hastings. Now used for great functions and for 'lying in State'.
No tours for security reasons; see also Houses of Parliament. *Station:* Westminster Cir.D.

*Whitechapel Art Gallery, Whitechapel High Street,   4E 67 A charitable trust founded to organise temporary exhibitions only. For details of exhibitions see daily press.
Open Tues. to Sun 11 a.m. to 5 p.m. Wed to 8 p.m.
Station: Aldgate East D.M.H.

Whitehall.   7B 74
Part of the original palace of Whitehall, this famous thoroughfare extends from Trafalgar Square southwards to Parliament Square. At the entrance to the Horse Guards Parade, mounted guards are on sentry duty. Downing Street, home of the Prime Minister, is a turning off Whitehall near the Cenotaph, the principal monument in the centre of the road. Many Government Departments are housed here.
Station: Charing Cross B.J.N.SR., Westminster Cir.D.

Windsor Castle, see page 38.

Winston Churchill's Britain at War Experience, 64/66 Tooley Street 4B78. Relive the drama of life during the Second World War; the Blitz comes alive with sound, smells and visual effects, experience how we lived through "those darkest days". *Admission Charge.* Open daily 10 a.m. to 4.30 p.m., until 5.30 p.m. Summer months. *Station:* London Bridge N.

PAGEANTRY

CEREMONY OF THE KEYS Tower of London, continues after 700 years to be a 10 p.m. nightly event. The Chief Yeoman Warder—in scarlet coat, Tudor bonnet, and carrying a lantern—with foot Guard escort, locks up the several gates. On approach to the Bloody Tower archway, a sentry challenges:

'Halt! Who comes there?'

'The Keys.'

'Whose Keys?'

'Queen Elizabeth's Keys.'

'Advance, Queen Elizabeth's Keys. All's well!'

Members of the public who have applied for (at least 2 months prior) and received permit may attend.

CHANGING OF THE GUARD

BUCKINGHAM PALACE. Takes place every morning at 11.30 (alternate days in winter). The ceremony is carried out by one of the five regiments of Foot Guards, marching to the band, and resplendent in scarlet tunics and black bearskins (cancelled in very wet weather). HORSE GUARDS Courtyard, Whitehall. Daily at 11 a.m. (Sundays, 10 a.m.) Ceremony by one of the two regiments of Household Cavalry, either the Royal Horse Guard in blue tunics, or the Life Guards in scarlet. Traditional breastplates are worn by both regiments.

LORD MAYOR'S SHOW. A colourful annual procession (usually second Saturday November) when the newly-elected Lord Mayor drives in his gilded state coach, drawn by six horses, to the Law Courts to take the oath.

MAUNDY THURSDAY. The Queen distributes purses of money to as many poor people as the years of her age.

OPENING OF THE ROYAL COURTS OF JUSTICE, Strand. The first Monday in October, all Her Majesty's Judges and members of the Bar—in State robes and full-bottomed wigs—attend a service in Westminster Abbey. Then, led by the Lord Chancellor, they walk in procession to the House of Lords; and, after lunching there, drive to the Law Courts. The first Motion of the year, taken in his court by the Lord Chancellor, constitutes the opening of all the courts.

REMEMBRANCE SUNDAY. Annually, on the Sunday nearest November 11th, the Queen, the Prime Minister, Ministers, and members of the Opposition, take up their places by the Cenotaph, for the 11 a.m. two minutes' silence. Then the Queen leads the laying of wreaths in memory of those killed in battle since 1914.

ROYAL TOURNAMENT. Annual display by the armed forces which takes place at Earls Court in June or July. One of the performances is normally attended by the Queen.

STATE OPENING OF PARLIAMENT. (After each General Election, and normally end October, beginning November.) The Queen, wearing her crown and robes of state, and escorted by Life Guards and Royal Horse Guards, drives in her state coach along the Mall and Whitehall to the Houses of Parliament. There, in the House of Lords, she makes her speech from the throne, before driving back to Buckingham Palace.

TROOPING THE COLOUR. Every June, on the Queen's official birthday, this ceremony—dating from 1750—takes place on the Horse Guards Parade. The Queen, accompanied by Household Cavalry, rides there from Buckingham Palace and back again, to the strains of martial music.

BRASS RUBBING CENTRES
St. Martin in the Fields, St. Martin's Place.2B 74 Open 10 a.m. to 6 p.m. Mon to Sat. 12 to 6 p.m. Sun.
All Hallows by the Tower, Byward St.   2C 78 Open 11 a.m. to 4 p.m. Sun. 1 p.m. to 4 p.m. Summer season only.
Westminster Abbey,   2B 86 Open 9 a.m. to 5 p.m. Mon. to Sat.

FLOODLIT PLACES OF INTEREST
Normally dusk to midnight April to Oct.
Admiralty Arch, Banqueting House, County Hall, Dover House (Whitehall), Guildhall, Gwydyr House (Whitehall), Horse Guards, Houses of Parliament, Jewel Tower (near Westminster Abbey), Mansion House, Marble Arch, National Gallery, Old Admiralty, Old Bailey, Old Scotland Yard (Victoria Embankment), Old War Office (Whitehall), Royal Courts of Justice, Royal Hospital Chelsea, Royal Naval College Greenwich, St. James's Park, St. Paul's Cathedral, Somerset House, South Bank Arts Centre, Tate Gallery, Tower of London, Trafalgar Square, Wellington Arch, Westminster Abbey and the following bridges—Albert, Chelsea, Lambeth, London, Vauxhall, Waterloo and Westminster.

TRIPS IN LONDON
Places in bold type appear in alphabetical order from page 2, together with description and admission times.
For COACH TOURS see page 39.
One day: Starting at **Buckingham Palace** a walk along Birdcage Walk brings you to Parliament Square, with **Westminster Abbey,** the **Houses of Parliament** and Big Ben. Leaving **Westminster Bridge** on the right, walk up **Whitehall** past **Downing Street** and the **Horse Guards** to

Trafalgar Square; where are Nelson's Column and the **National Gallery**. If your interests are historical and architectural take a bus along the **Strand** past the Law Courts to **Fleet Street** and **St. Paul's Cathedral**, and from there a bus to the **Monument**. A walk along Eastcheap and Great Tower Street brings you to the **Tower of London**.

If you prefer to see the West End shopping centre, take a bus from **Trafalgar Square** through **Piccadilly Circus**, up **Regent Street** to Oxford Circus. Walk west along **Oxford Street** to **Bond Street**, and down **Bond Street**.

Two days: Take the underground to Tower Hill, and nearby is the **Tower of London** with **Tower Bridge** beyond. Across the river are seen **H.M.S. Belfast** and the spires of **Southwark Cathedral**.

A walk along Lower Thames Street and through **Billingsgate Fish Market** brings you to the **Monument**, from which King William Street leads to the heart of the City, with the **Bank of England**, the **Mansion House** and the **Royal Exchange** among many other famous buildings. From here, **St. Paul's Cathedral** is a short bus ride or walk. Almost any bus going down Ludgate Hill continues through the newspaper world of **Fleet Street** to the **Strand**. On the right are the Law Courts, and in the middle of the road the island churches of St. Clement Danes and St. Mary-le-Strand.

The **Strand** opens into **Trafalgar Square**, with its fountains, Nelson's Column, **Admiralty Arch** and the **National Gallery**. Any bus down **Whitehall** passes the entrance to the **Horse Guards** where two mounted sentries are on guard. On the left is Inigo Jones's **Banqueting House**, from which Charles I was led to his execution. Government offices line **Whitehall**, and on the right is the famous **Downing Street**. The **Cenotaph** is slightly beyond and soon **Whitehall** opens out into Parliament Square.

Here, the **Houses of Parliament**, St. Margaret's Church and **Westminster Abbey** form an impressive group. Take a bus proceeding along Victoria Street—on the right is the **New Scotland Yard** building—to Victoria Station; on the left rises the Campanile of **Westminster Cathedral**, and walk along Buckingham Palace Road to **Buckingham Palace**, where the standard will be flying if Her Majesty the Queen is in residence. Walk along the tree-lined Mall and skirt the battlemented walls of **St. James's Palace**—the home of the Duke of Windsor while Prince of Wales. Pall Mall, with its well-known clubs, is soon reached. Farther along Pall Mall is **Waterloo Place**, with the **Duke of York's Column** in the centre and on the left, **Piccadilly Circus**. A bus up **Regent Street** to Oxford Circus, and another along **Oxford Street** to Museum Street, brings you near to the **British Museum.** From here it is only a short distance to London University.

Three days: The same route should be followed, but more time devoted to the **Tower of London**, **St. Paul's**

Cathedral, the **National Gallery** in **Trafalgar Square**, **Westminster Abbey** and the **British Museum**. Then take the Central Line underground from Tottenham Court Road to Queensway, and walk south along the Broad Walk through **Kensington Gardens**. On the right lies **Kensington Palace**, on the left the Round Pond. On reaching Kensington Road turn left to the **Albert Memorial**, the **Royal Albert Hall** and the museums: the **Science Museum**, the **Natural History Museum**, and the **Victoria and Albert Museum**. Close by is the Roman Catholic Brompton **Oratory** and the busy shopping centres of Brompton Road and Knightsbridge.

Four or more days: More time should be given to the places already mentioned that interest you most; but while in the **Strand**, **Lincoln's Inn Fields** and the **Temple** should be visited. It is a short walk to the **Victoria Embankment** to see the fine stretch of river with gardens, statues and monuments.

A short distance from **Oxford Street**, opposite Bond Street Station, is the **Wallace Collection** in Manchester Square. From Baker Street, nearby, buses go to **Regent's Park**, with its **London Zoo.**

TRIPS OUT OF CENTRAL LONDON

*CHARTWELL (01732 866368) near Westerham, Kent, was for many years the country home of Sir Winston Churchill. Many of his paintings were done here. Open to the public since his death, it continues to be one of the most visited places in England. Now a National Trust Property. Alternate Green Line 705 from Victoria Coach Station runs via Chartwell, Summer season only (0181 668 7261).

*GREENWICH is world famous for the OLD ROYAL OBSERVATORY (0181-858 4422) founded in 1675 by Charles II on high ground overlooking the Royal Park laid out by Le Notre. The Observatory, incorporating Wren's Flamsteed House, the 'Greenwich Mean Time' time ball, zero meridian of longitude mark and planetarium summer shows, is part of the NATIONAL MARITIME MUSEUM (0181-858 4422). The museum has exhibits ranging from ships models to actual boats, galleries devoted to Admiral Nelson and the Battle of Trafalgar, Captain Cook, the Royal Navy, shipbuilding, navigation, exploration, archaeology, etc. and contains many fine paintings. The museum also incorporates the QUEEN'S HOUSE commissioned by James I, built 1619–37 to designs by Inigo Jones, and with his Banqueting House (page 3) was a forerunner of classical architecture in England. Facing the river stands the ROYAL NAVAL COLLEGE (0181-858 2154) built on the site of the Royal Palace of Placentia, a favourite residence of the Tudor monarchs; the Painted Hall and Chapel are open to the public. Nearby are CUTTY SARK (0181-858 3445) the last and fastest of the famous tea clippers, launched in 1869; and GIPSY MOTH IV, in which Sir Francis Chichester made his solo world voyage.

Station: Greenwich or Maze Hill from Charing Cross SR.; or Maze Hill from Cannon Street SR. In summer, by boat from Westminster, Charing Cross or Tower Piers. Dockland Light Railway then foot tunnel under Thames.

*HAMPTON COURT PALACE (0181-781 9500), built by Cardinal Wolsey in 1515, and at that time the largest and most magnificent palace in England, it aroused Henry VIII's envy and concern. Ten years later it was presented to him by the Cardinal, and from then until George II, remained a favourite royal residence. It contains many fine paintings and tapestries. The grounds and gardens, with the Orangery by Wren and the famous Maze, were laid out by William III.
Station: Hampton Court, from Waterloo SR. In summer, by boat from Westminster Pier.

*KEW GARDENS (ROYAL BOTANIC GARDENS, 0181-940 1171), Kew, beautifully situated by the Thames, contain over 25,000 different species and varieties of trees, shrubs and plants from all over the world. There are two museums, a Palm House, Lily House, Rhododendron Walk, etc.
Station: Kew Gardens D., Kew Bridge from Waterloo SR. In summer, by boat from Westminster Pier.

*WINDSOR CASTLE (01753 868286), Berkshire. Since William the Conqueror's wood and earth castle, a royal residence. When Her Majesty, Queen Elizabeth is here, the Royal Standard flies from the Round Tower. The State Apartments, rebuilt by Charles II, and richly furnished, contain works of art by the Old Masters. St. George's Chapel—a fine example of Perpendicular architecture—was begun for Edward IV as a private chapel for Knights of the Garter. Windsor Great Park with its famous Long Walk, and Virginia Water, is all that remains of the ancient Royal Forest of Windsor.
Station: Windsor and Eton Central from Paddington WR. Windsor and Eton Riverside from Waterloo SR.

TOURIST INFORMATION CENTRES
British Travel Centre 12 Regent St.   2F 73 Open: 9 a.m. to 6.30 p.m. Mon. to Fri. 10 a.m. to 5 p.m. Sat. & Sun.
City of London Information Centre St. Pauls Churchyard   5D 64 0171-606 3030 Open: daily 9.30 a.m. to 5 p.m. April to Sept. Winter months 9.30 to 5 p.m. Mon to Fri., to 12 noon Sun. Closed Sun.
Discover Islington Visitor Centre 44 Duncan St. NI 0171-278 8787 Open: 11 a.m. to 5 p.m. Mon. to Sat. (10 a.m. to 5 p.m. Summer Season.)
Docklands Visitor Centre 3 Limeharbour E14 0171-512 3000 Open: 9 a.m. to 6 p.m. Mon. to Fri. 10.30 a.m. to 4.30 p.m. Sat. & Sun.
Greenwich Tourist Information Centre 46 Greenwich Church St. SE10 0181-858 6376 Open: daily 10.15 a.m. to 4.45 p.m.

Heathrow Central Underground Concourse Heathrow
Airport Open Daily 8.30 a.m. to 6 p.m.
Liverpool Street Underground Station 3B 66 Open:
8.15 a.m. to 7 p.m. Mon. to 6 p.m. Tues. to Sat. 8.30 a.m.
to 5.45 p.m. Sun.
Selfridges Department Store Basement Arcade, Duke
Street entrance 5A 60 Open: Store hours.
Victoria Station Tourist Information Centre 3C 84
Open: daily 8 a.m. to 7 p.m. Easter to Oct. reduced hours
in Winter season.

LONDON TOURIST BOARD PHONE GUIDE
01839 123 456. For full guide see page 48.

THAMES RIVER TRIPS
For river boat information see telephone guide p. 48.
FROM WESTMINSTER PIER 1C 86: CHARING CROSS
PIER 3D 75
Regular trips to Tower of London, Greenwich and Thames
Barrier downstream (details 0171-930 4097); also services
to Kew Gardens, Richmond and Hampton Court upstream
(details 0171-930 2062).
FROM TOWER PIER 3C 78
Regular trips to Greenwich and Thames Barrier downstream
(details 0171-488 0344); and Westminster upstream (details
0171-488 0344); also across the river to HMS *Belfast*.

CANAL TRIPS
JASON'S TRIP & ARGONAUT GALLERY 2D 57
Little Venice, W2. For bookings, telephone 0171-286 3428.
*JENNY WREN CANAL TRIPS
Camden High St., NW1. For bookings telephone 0171-485
6210.
LONDON WATERBUS COMPANY 2D 57
Little Venice, W2. and Camden Lock. 0171-482 2550.

TRANSPORT INFORMATION
London Transport 24 hr. information service 0171-222
1234.
SPECIAL TOURIST FACILITIES
ROUND LONDON SIGHTSEEING TOUR
This circular tour of the landmarks of London lasting
approximately 2 hours covers 20 miles of the West End
and City. It is possible to board the buses at four places;
Baker Street Station 2E 59, Marble Arch 1E 71, Pic-
cadilly Circus (Haymarket) 2F 73, and Victoria 3C 84.
CONDUCTED COACH TOURS
Tours are guide conducted in luxury coaches to some of
the famous show places in and around London. All seats
bookable. For information and to reserve seats apply to
London Transport Travel Enquiry Offices, Victoria Coach
Station or travel agents.
TRAVELCARDS
Travelcards are on sale at Underground Stations, London

Transport Travel Information Centres, British Rail Stations and London Tourist Board Centres.

Travelcards give access to London Transport buses and Underground trains, also the Docklands Light Railway and parts of the British Rail system. Travelcards are good value, save time as well as the need to buy separate tickets for each journey. Travelcards can be bought for 1 day or 7 days (photograph required for 7 days). They cannot be used on coach tours.

BUSES AND UNDERGROUND RAILWAY

These are operated by the London Regional Transport, whose headquarters are at 55 Broadway, Westminster, SW1. Tel.: 0171-222 1234. For Underground Map see back cover.

TRAVEL INFORMATION CENTRES: St. James's Park, Euston, King's Cross, Oxford Circus, Piccadilly Circus, Victoria and Heathrow Central Underground Stations. Also Waterloo BR.

AIRBUS: A direct bus service between Heathrow Airport and central London, A1 Terminus—Grosvenor Gardens, SW1   3B 84, A2 Terminus—Russell Square   1B 62 via Euston Station   4F 53.

COACHES

Victoria Coach Station, 164 Buckingham Palace Road
Tel.: 0171-730 0202   5B 84

FLIGHTLINE 767, National Bus Co., direct service linking Victoria Coach Station and Heathrow Airport.

FLIGHTLINE 777 direct service linking Gatwick Airport and Victoria (Buckingham Pal. Rd.)

FLIGHTLINE 757 direct service linking Luton Airport and Victoria (Eccleston Bridge).

DOCKLANDS LIGHT RAILWAY

From Bank Station   1A 78 or Tower Gateway Station   1E 79 to Isle of Dogs serving West India Docks/Canary Wharf and Millwall Docks development areas Bus service at weekends.

MAIN LINE RAILWAY TERMINI

EASTERN REGION

King's Cross   2B 54 Tel.: 0171-278 2477; Fenchurch St.
1C 78 and Liverpool St.   3B 66.
Tel.: 0171-928 5100.

LONDON MIDLAND REGION Tel.: 0171-387 7070
Euston   3E 53, Marylebone   1C 58, St. Pancras   2B 54.

SOUTHERN REGION Tel.: 0171-928 5100
Blackfriars   1C 76, Cannon Street   1F 77, Charing Cross   3C 74, London Bridge   7A 78, Victoria   7C 84, Waterloo   5F 75.

WESTERN REGION Tel.: 0171-262 6767
Paddington   4F 57.

Note: Tickets for any station, irrespective of region, may be obtained from any of the above stations. Seats and sleeping berths may be reserved in the same way.

RED ARROW BUSES link Waterloo, Victoria, Liverpool Street, Charing Cross, Holborn Viaduct and London Bridge Stations with the City and West End. They provide fast and frequent services for peak hour travellers and shoppers.

EUROSTAR
Waterloo International   5E 75 Through services direct to Paris and Brussels via the Channel Tunnel.

TAXIS
Scale of charges is shown in each taxi-cab.

LOST PROPERTY OFFICES
BUSES, UNDERGROUND and on LONDON TRANSPORT EXECUTIVE PROPERTY: 200 Baker St., NW1. (No enquiries regarding Lost Property answered by phone.)
OTHER LOST PROPERTY: Metropolitan Police Lost Property Office: 15 Penton St., N1.
MAINLINE RAILWAYS: At the Terminal Station of the Main Line concerned.

PLACES OF WORSHIP
BAPTIST
BLOOMSBURY CENTRAL CHURCH, Shaftesbury Avenue.   4B 62 *Station:* Tottenham Court Road
GOWER STREET MEMORIAL CHAPEL, Shaftesbury Avenue.   5B 62 *Station:* Tottenham Court Road
METROPOLITAN TABERNACLE, Elephant & Castle, SE1.   4C 88 *Station:* Elephant & Castle
WESTMINSTER, Horseferry Road   3A 86 *Station:* St. James's Park

CHRISTIAN SCIENCE
FIRST CHURCH OF CHRIST, SCIENTIST, Sloane Terrace.   4F 83 *Station:* Sloane Square
THIRD CHURCH OF CHRIST, SCIENTIST, Curzon Street.   3B 72 *Station:* Green Park
NINTH CHURCH OF CHRIST, SCIENTIST, Marsham Street.   3A 86 *Station:* St. James's Park
ELEVENTH CHURCH OF CHRIST, SCIENTIST, 1 Nutford Place.   4D 59 *Station:* Marble Arch

CHURCH OF ENGLAND
ALL SAINTS, Margaret St.   4D 61 *Station:* Oxford Circus
ALL SOULS, Langham Place. 3C 60 *Station:* Oxford Circus
CHAPEL ROYAL, St. James's Palace.   4E 73
Station: Green Park
CHRIST CHURCH, Commercial St.   2D 67
Station: Aldgate East
ST. GEORGE (Hanover Square), St. George Street. 1C 72
Station: Oxford Circus
ST. GILES-IN-THE-FIELD, St. Giles High Street.   4A 62
Station: Tottenham Court Road
ST. JAMES'S, Piccadilly.   2E 73
Station: Piccadilly Circus
ST. MARGARET'S, Westminster.   1B 86
Station: Westminster

ST. MARTIN-IN-THE-FIELDS, St. Martin's Place. 2B 74
Station: Charing Cross
ST. MARYLEBONE, Marylebone Road. 1A 60
Station: Baker Street
ST. PAUL'S, Covent Garden. 1C 74
Station: Covent Garden (closed Sundays)
ST. PAUL'S CATHEDRAL, Ludgate Hill. 5C 64
Station: St. Paul's
SOUTHWARK CATHEDRAL, Cathedral St. 3F 77
Station: London Bridge
WESTMINSTER ABBEY 2B 86
Station: Westminster

CHURCH OF SCOTLAND
CROWN COURT CHURCH, Russell Street. 5C 62
Station: Holborn
ST. COLUMBA'S, Pont Street. 3D 86
Stations: Knightsbridge, Sloane Square

DANISH CHURCH
DANISH CHURCH, Regent's Park 2B 52
Station: Regent's Park

DUTCH CHURCH
DUTCH CHURCH, Austin Friars. 4A 66
Station: Bank

FRENCH PROTESTANT
EGLISE PROTESTANTE, FRANÇAISE DE LONDRES, 9
Soho Square. 4F 61
Station: Tottenham Court Road

GREEK ORTHODOX
ST. SOPHIA'S, Moscow Rd., 1B 68
Station: Bayswater

INDEPENDENT EVANGELICAL
WESTMINSTER CHAPEL, Buckingham Gate. 2E 85
Station: St. James's Park

INTERDENOMINATIONAL
AMERICAN CHURCH IN LONDON, 79 Tottenham Court
Road, 2E 61 *Station:* Goodge Street

JEWISH
CENTRAL SYNAGOGUE, Gt. Portland Street. 2C 60
Station: Gt. Portland Street
NEW WEST END SYNAGOGUE, 10 St. Petersburgh
Place. 2B 68
Station: Queensway
SPANISH AND PORTUGUESE SYNAGOGUE, Bevis
Marks. 4C 66
Station: Aldgate
*SPANISH AND PORTUGUESE SYNAGOGUE, St.
James's Gardens, W11.
Station: Holland Park
WEST LONDON SYNAGOGUE (Reform), 34 Upper Berk-
eley Street. 5D 59
Station: Marble Arch

LUTHERAN
ST. ANNE & ST. AGNES (LUTHERAN) CHURCH, Gresham
Street.   4D 65
Station: St. Paul's

METHODIST
CENTRAL HALL, Westminster.   1A 86
Stations: Westminster, St. James's Park
CHILTERN STREET WELSH METHODIST, Chiltern
Street.   2F 59
Station: Baker Street
(Last Sunday in month 6.30 pm only)
HINDE STREET CHURCH, Theyer St.,   4A 60
Station: Bond Street
WESLEY'S CHAPEL, City Road.   1A 66 *Station:* Moorgate

MOSLEM
LONDON CENTRAL MOSQUE, Regent's Park.   4C 50
Station: Baker Street

ROMAN CATHOLIC
CHURCH OF THE IMMACULATE CONCEPTION, Farm
Street, Berkeley Square.   2B 72
Stations: Green Park, Bond Street
FRENCH CATHOLIC CHURCH OF NOTRE DAME DE
FRANCE, Leicester Place off Leicester Sq.   1A 74
Station: Leicester Square
ORATORY, THE, Brompton Road.   3B 82
Station: South Kensington
OUR LADY OF THE ASSUMPTION AND ST. GREGORY,
Warwick St.   1E 73 *Station:* Piccadilly Circus
*ST. BONIFACE GERMAN CATHOLIC CHURCH, Adler
Street, E1. *Station:* Aldgate East
ST. GEORGE'S CATHEDRAL, St. George's Road.   2A 88
Station: Lambeth North
ST. JAMES'S, Spanish Place, Manchester Square.   3A 60
Station: Bond Street
ST. PATRICK CATHOLIC CHURCH, 21 Soho Square.   5A
62
Station: Tottenham Court Road
UKRANIAN CATHOLIC CATHEDRAL, Duke Street. 1A 72
Station: Bond Street
WESTMINSTER CATHEDRAL, Ashley Place.   3D 85
Station: Victoria

RUSSIAN ORTHODOX CHURCH IN EXILE
ALL SAINTS CATHEDRAL, Ennismore Gardens, SW7. 1B
82
Station: South Kensington

SALVATION ARMY
REGENT HALL, 275 Oxford Street.   5C 60
Station: Oxford Circus

SOCIETY OF FRIENDS (QUAKERS)
FRIENDS HOUSE, Euston Road.   5F 53

Station: Euston Square
TOYNBEE HALL, 28 Commercial Street.   3E 67
Station: Aldgate East
WESTMINSTER MEETING HOUSE, 52 St. Martin's Lane.
1B 74
Station: Leicester Square

SWEDISH
SWEDISH CHURCH, 11 Harcourt Street.   3C 58
Stations: Edgware Road, Marylebone

SWISS CHURCH
EGLISE SUISSE DE LONDRES, 79 Endell Street.   4B 62
Station: Tottenham Court Road

UNITARIAN
ESSEX CHURCH, Palace Gardens Terrace,   3A 68
Station: Notting Hill Gate

UNITED REFORMED
CHRIST CHURCH AND UPTON CHAPEL, Westminster
Bridge Road.   2E 87 *Station:* Lambeth North
CITY TEMPLE, Holborn Viaduct.   3A 64 *Station:* St. Paul's
REGENT SQUARE, Regent Square.   4C 54
Stations: King's Cross, St. Pancras
ST. JOHN'S CHURCH, Allen Street,   2A 80
Station: High Street, Kensington

WELSH
*WELSH PRESBYTERIAN CHURCH, 265 Willesden La.
NW2.
Station: Willesden Green
*Outside Central London area mapped.

WEST END CINEMAS
Nearest station shown in italics. ‡*Membership only*
BARBICAN 1 Silk St.   2E 65 *Barbican, Moorgate*
*CHELSEA CINEMA 206 King's Rd., SW3. *Sloane Square*
CURZON MAYFAIR Curzon St.   4B 72 *Green Park*
CURZON PHOENIX Charing Cross Rd.   5A 62 *Tottenham
   Court Rd.*
CURZON WEST END Shaftesbury Av.   5A 62 *Piccadilly
   Circus*
DOMINION Tottenham Ct. Rd.   4A 62 *Tottenham Ct. Rd.*
*ELECTRIC 191 Portobello Rd. *Notting Hill Gate*
EMPIRE Leicester Square.   1A 74 *Leicester Square*
‡ICA Nash Ho., The Mall.   3A 74 *Charing Cross*
LUMIERE St. Martin's La.   2B 74 *Leicester Square*
METRO Rupert Street.   1F 73 *Piccadilly Circus*
MEZZANINE, see Odeon Leicester Square
MGM Baker St.   1E 59 *Baker St.*
MGM CHELSEA 279 King's Rd. SW3. *Sloane Sq.*
MGM Haymarket.   2F 73 *Piccadilly Circus*
MGM Oxford Street.   4A 62 *Tottenham Ct. Rd.*
MGM Panton St.   2A 74 *Piccadilly Circus.*

44

MGM PICCADILLY CIRCUS, Piccadilly, W1. 2E 73
  Piccadilly Circus
MGM PREMIERE Swiss Centre, 1F 73 *Leicester Square*
MGM Shaftesbury Avenue, 5A 62 *Leicester Square*
MGM Tottenham Ct. Rd. 3F 61 *Tottenham Ct. Rd.*
MGM TROCADERO, Trocadero Centre. 2F 73 *Piccadilly
  Circus*
MINEMA 45 Knightsbridge. 5F 71 *Hyde Park Corner*
MOMI Museum of the Moving Image, South Bank. 3E
  75 *Waterloo*
‡NATIONAL FILM THEATRE South Bank. 3E 75 *Waterloo*
*ODEON HAMMERSMITH, Queen Caroline St. W6
  Hammersmith
ODEON Haymarket. 2F 73 *Piccadilly Circus*
ODEON Kensington High Street. 2A 80 *High Street
  Kensington*
ODEON LEICESTER SQUARE. 2A 74 *Leicester Square*
ODEON WEST END Leicester Square. 2A 74 *Leicester
  Square*
ODEON Marble Arch. 5E 59 *Marble Arch*
PLAZA 1 & 2 Lwr. Regent St. 2F 73 *Piccadilly Circus*
PRINCE CHARLES Leicester Sq. 1A 74 *Leicester Square*
RENOIR, Brunswick Square. 1C 62 *Russell Square*
SCREEN ON BAKER ST. Baker St. 2E 59 *Baker St.*
*SCREEN ON THE GREEN Islington Green, N1. *Angel*
UCI Whiteleys Centre, Queensway. 5C 56 *Queensway*
WARNER WEST END Leicester Square. 1A 74 *Leicester
  Square*
*Outside Central London area mapped.

WEST END THEATRES, BALLET AND OPERA HOUSES

‡Membership only
*Outside Central London area mapped.
ADELPHI Strand. 2C 74 *Charing Cross*
ALBERY St. Martins La. 1B 74 *Leicester Square*
ALDWYCH Aldwych. 1D 75 *Covent Garden*
AMBASSADORS West St. 5B 62 *Leicester Square*
APOLLO Shaftesbury Av. 1F 73 *Piccadilly Circus*
APOLLO VICTORIA Wilton Rd. 3D 85 *Victoria*
‡ARTS 6 Gt. Newport St. 1B 74 *Leicester Square*
ASTORIA Charing Cross Rd. 4A 62 *Tottenham Ct. Rd.*
BARBICAN Silk St. 2E 65 *Barbican, Moorgate*
BLOOMSBURY Gordon St. 5F 53. *Euston Square*
BRITTEN OPERA THEATRE, Ryl. Coll. of Music, Prince
  Consort Rd. 2F 81 *South Kensington*
CAMBRIDGE Earlham St. 5B 62 *Leicester Square*
COCKPIT Gateforth St. 1B 58 *Marylebone*
COLISEUM St. Martin's Lane. 2B 74 *Leicester Square*
COMEDY Panton St. 2A 74 *Piccadilly Circus*
CRITERION Piccadilly. 2F 73 *Piccadilly Circus*
DOMINION, Tottenham Ct. Rd. 4A 62 *Tottenham Ct. Rd.*
DONMAR WAREHOUSE see *Warehouse*

DRURY LANE Catherine St.   5D 63 *Covent Garden*
DUCHESS Catherine St.   1D 75 *Covent Garden*
DUKE OF YORK'S St. Martin's Lane.   2B 74 *Leicester Square*
ENGLISH NATIONAL OPERA, see Coliseum
FORTUNE Russell St.   5C 62 *Covent Garden*
GARRICK Charing Cross Rd.   2B 74 *Leicester Square*
GIELGUD Shaftesbury Av.   1F 73 *Piccadilly Circus*
HAYMARKET Haymarket.   3F 73 *Piccadilly Circus*
HER MAJESTY'S Haymarket.   3F 73 *Piccadilly Circus*
‡ICA Carlton Ho. Ter.   3A 74 *Charing Cross*
JEANETTA COCHRANE Southampton Row. 3D 63 *Holborn*
LYRIC Shaftesbury Av.   1F 73 *Piccadilly Circus*
*LYRIC HAMMERSMITH King St., W6 *Hammersmith*
MAYFAIR Stratton St.   3C 72 *Green Park*
MERMAID Puddle Dock.   1C 76 *Blackfriars*
NATIONAL South Bank.   3E 75 *Waterloo*
NEW LONDON Drury La.   5D 63 *Covent Garden*
OLD VIC Waterloo Rd.   5A 76 *Waterloo*
OPEN AIR Regent's Park.   4F 51 *Baker St.*
PALACE Shaftesbury Av.   5A 62 *Leicester Square*
PALLADIUM 8 Argyll St.   5D 61 *Oxford Circus*
PHOENIX Charing Cross Rd.   5A 62 *Tottenham Ct. Rd.*
PICCADILLY Denman St.   1E 73 *Piccadilly Circus*
‡PLAYERS' Villiers St.   3C 74 *Embankment*
PLAYHOUSE, Northumberland Avenue,   3C 74 *Charing Cross*
PORTCULLIS Monck St.   3A 86 *St. James's Park*
PRINCE EDWARD Old Compton St.   5F 61 *Leicester Square*
PRINCE OF WALES Coventry St. 2F 73 *Piccadilly Circus*
QUEENS Shaftesbury Av.   1F 73 *Piccadilly Circus*
‡RAYMOND REVUEBAR Brewer St. 1F 73 *Piccadilly Circus*
ROYAL COURT Sloane Square.   5F 83 *Sloane Square*
ROYAL OPERA HOUSE Covent Garden.   5C 62 *Covent Garden*
ROYALTY Kingsway.   5D 63 *Holborn (Kingsway)*
*SADLER'S WELLS Rosebery Av. *Angel*
ST. MARTIN'S West St.   1B 74 *Leicester Square*
SAVOY Strand.   2D 75 *Embankment*
SHAFTESBURY Shaftesbury Av. 4B 62 *Tottenham Ct. Rd.*
SHAW Euston Rd.   3A 54 *King's Cross*
STRAND Aldwych.   1D 75 *Covent Garden*
THEATRE ROYAL Drury Lane, see Drury Lane
THEATRE ROYAL Haymarket, see Haymarket
*THEATRE ROYAL Stratford East, Gerry Raffles Sq., E15 *Stratford*
VAUDEVILLE Strand.   2C 74 *Embankment*
VICTORIA PALACE Victoria St.   3C 84 *Victoria*
WAREHOUSE Earlham St.   5B 62 *Leicester Square*
WESTMINSTER Palace St.   2D 85 *Victoria*
WHITEHALL 14 Whitehall.   3B 74 *Charing Cross*
WYNDHAM'S Charing Cross Rd. 1B 74 *Leicester Square*

YOUNG VIC 66 The Cut.   5A 76 *Waterloo*

CONCERT HALLS
BARBICAN HALL Silk St.   2E 65 *Barbican, Moorgate*
CENTRAL HALL Tothill St.   1A 86 *St. James's Park*
CONWAY HALL Red Lion Sq. 2D 63 *Holborn (Kingsway)*
GUILDHALL SCHOOL OF MUSIC & DRAMA
   Barbican.   2E 65 *Barbican, Moorgate*
LOGAN HALL; Inst. of Education, 20 Bedford Way.   1A
   62 *Russell Square*
PURCELL ROOM South Bank.   3E 75 *Waterloo*
QUEEN ELIZABETH HALL South Bank. 3E 75 *Waterloo*
ROYAL ALBERT HALL Kensington Gore.   1F 81 *South
   Kensington*
ROYAL COLLEGE OF MUSIC Prince Consort Rd.   2F 81
   South Kensington
ROYAL FESTIVAL HALL South Bank.   4E 75 *Waterloo*
ST. JOHN'S Smith Square.   3B 86 *Westminster*
*SADLER'S WELLS Rosebery Av.   *Angel*
WEMBLEY ARENA Empire Way, Wembley. *Wembley Park*
WIGMORE HALL 36 Wigmore St.   4B 60 *Bond St. Oxford
   Circus*
*Outside Central London area mapped.

GOVERNMENT OFFICES
Admiralty (Old Building) –
   4A 74
Commonwealth Office –
   5B 74
Department of the
   Environment – 3A 86
Foreign Office – 5B 74
Home Office – 1F 85
Houses of Parliament – 1C 86
Land Registry – 4E 63
Ministry of Defence –
   4C 74
Northern Ireland Office –
   1B 86
Passport Office – 2E 85
Patent Office – 3E 63
Public Record Office –
   4F 63
Scottish Office – 5B 74
Treasury – 5B 74
Welsh Office – 5B 74

SHOPS
Army and Navy Stores – 3E 85
Austin Reed – 2D 73
C and A – 4D 61/1F 71
Debenhams – 5B 60
D. H. Evans – 5B 60
Dickins and Jones – 5D 61
Fenwick – 1C 72
Fortnum and Mason – 3E 73
Foyle's – 5A 62
Geographers' A-Z Map
   Company – 2F 63
Hamleys – 1D 73
Harrods – 2D 83
Harvey Nichols – 1E 83
Heals – 2F 61
Littlewoods – 5F 59
London Pavilion – 2F 73
Mappin and Webb – 1D 73
Marks and Spencer (Marble
   Arch) – 5F 59
Marks and Spencer (Oxford
   Circus) – 5D 61
Peter Jones – 5E 83
Peter Robinson – 4D 61
Selfridges – 5A 60
Simpsons – 2E 73
Thomas Neal's – 5B 62
Trocadero Centre – 1F 73
West London Silver
   Vaults – 3F 63

John Lewis – 5C 60
Liberty – 5D 61

Whiteleys Centre – 3A
54/5B 56

AUCTIONEERS
Bonham and Sons – 2C 82
Christies – 3E 73/5F 81

Phillips – 5B 60
Sotheby's – 1C 72

LONDON TOURIST BOARD
TELEPHONE GUIDE

Dial 0839 123 plus
the last three numbers as shown

PLACES TO VISIT

Popular Attractions	480	Military & Maritime History	482
Museums	429	Famous Houses & Gardens	483
Palaces, Royal & State	481	Day Trips from London	484

WHERE TO TAKE CHILDREN

What's On	404	Places to Visit	424

WHAT'S ON

What's on this Week	400	Major Sporting Events	405
Sunday in London	407	Rock & Pop Concerts	422
Current Exhibitions	403	Summer in the Parks	406

SPECIAL EVENTS

Changing the Guard	411	Chelsea Flower Show	412
Lord Mayor's Show,		London Marathon	414
State Opening of Parliament		Wimbledon Tennis	417
& Trooping the Colour	413	Christmas & Easter	418

THEATRE

Comedy & Thrillers	415	Non West End Productions	434
Musicals	416	New Productions, How to	
Shakespeare	419	Book	438
Plays	425		

OUT & ABOUT

Getting around London	430	Shopping in London	486
Guided Tours & Walks	431	Street Markets	428
River Trips	432	Pubs & Restaurants	485
Getting to the Airports	433		

ACCOMMODATION

General Advice	435
Bookings Hotline 0171 824 8844	

WEATHER

Met Office Forecast for	
Greater London	0839 500 951

Note: Calls cost 36p per minute cheap rate, 48p per minute at all other times plus any hotel/payphone surcharge.

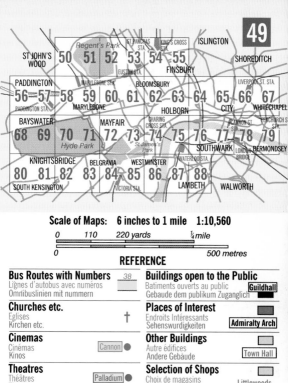

Map Index Grid (Page 49)

ST JOHN'S WOOD	**Regent's Park**		ST PANCRAS STA.	KING'S CROSS STA.	ISLINGTON
					SHOREDITCH
50	**51**	**52**	**53**	**54 55**	FINSBURY
		EUSTON STA.			
PADDINGTON	MARYLEBONE STA.		BLOOMSBURY		LIVERPOOL ST. STA.
56 57 58	**59**	**60 61**	**62 63 64**	**65 66 67**	WHITECHAPEL
PADDINGTON STA.	MARYLEBONE		HOLBORN	CITY	
BAYSWATER		MAYFAIR	CHARING CROSS STA.	CANNON ST. STA.	FENCHURCH S. STA.
68 69	**70 71**	**72 73**	**74 75**	**76 77 78 79**	
	Hyde Park	St James's Park		SOUTHWARK	LONDON BRIDGE, BERMONDSEY
KNIGHTSBRIDGE	BELGRAVIA	WESTMINSTER	WATERLOO STA.		
80 81 82	**83 84 85**	**86 87 88**			
SOUTH KENSINGTON	VICTORIA STA.	LAMBETH	WALWORTH		

49

Scale of Maps: 6 inches to 1 mile   1:10,560

```
0      110     220 yards        ¼ mile
0                              500 metres
```

REFERENCE

Bus Routes with Numbers *38*
Lignes d'autobus avec numéros
Omnibuslinien mit nummern

Churches etc. †
Eglises
Kirchen etc.

Cinemas `Cannon` ●
Cinémas
Kinos

Theatres `Palladium` ●
Théâtres
Theater

Embassies, Legations etc. Mexico ☀
Embassades, Légations etc.
Botschaften Gesandschaften etc.

Hospitals St Pancras Hospital ⊞
Hôpitaux
Krankenhaüser

Hotels Dorchester ★
Hôtels
Hotels

Information Centres 𝒊
Syndicat d'initiatives
Informationsstellen

Buildings open to the Public `Guildhall`
Batiments ouverts au public
Gebäude dem publikum Zuganglich

Places of Interest `Admiralty Arch`
Endroits Intéressants
Sehenswurdigkeiten

Other Buildings `Town Hall`
Autre édifices
Andere Gebäude

Selection of Shops Littlewoods
Choix de magasins
Auswahl Von Läden

Toilets ▽
Toilettes
Toiletten

Main Line Stations `EUSTON`
Gares de Lignes principales
Bahnhofe

Underground Stations ⊖ `Angel`
Stations de métro
U Bahn

Docklands Light Railway `DLR` `Bank`
train léger des Docklands
Docklands L-Bahn

Ⓒ **Edition 22 1996**

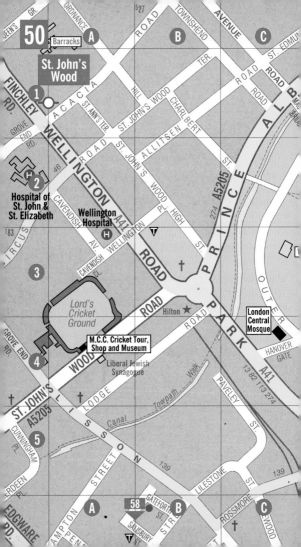

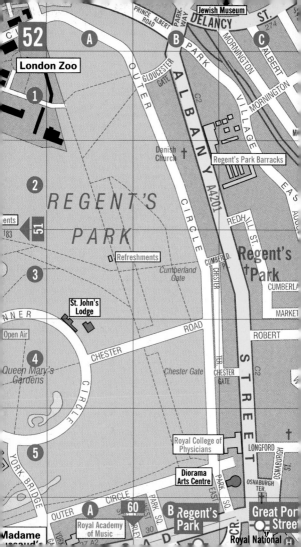

52

(A)   (B)   (C)

London Zoo

1

PRINCE ALBERT ROAD

Jewish Museum

DELANCY   **ST.**

274

PARKWAY

GLOUCESTER GATE

OUTER

MORNINGTON

ALBERT

VILLAGE

MORNINGTON

2

REGENT'S

Danish Church

C2

Regent's Park Barracks

A4201

51

183

PARK

CIRCLE

REDHILL ST.

Regent's Park

Refreshments

Cumberland Gate

3

CUMBERLAND RD.

CHESTER

CUMBERL

MARKET

INNER

St. John's Lodge

Open Air

ROAD

ROBERT

4

CHESTER

S

T

R

E

E

T

Queen Mary's Gardens

CIRCLE

Chester Gate

CHESTER GATE

TER.

C2

5

Royal College of Physicians

LONGFORD

OSNABURGH ST.

YORK BRIDGE

Diorama Arts Centre

PARK EAST

SQ.

OSNABURGH TER.

Madame
ussaud's

OUTER

CIRCLE

(A) **Royal Academy of Music**

YORK

27 A2

60

PARK SQ.

30

(B) **Regent's Park**

CR.

Great Por
Street

Royal National

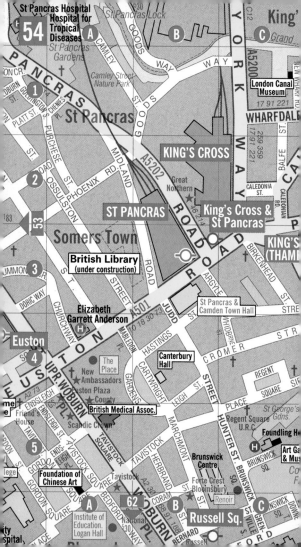

This is a map of the Pentonville and Clerkenwell area.

Cross

D · Canal · CARNEGIE ST · E · CHARLOTTE · RD · COPENHAGEN ST · F · LIVERPOOL

55

17 91 259 35 · 153

CLOUDESLEY RD · 1

MARKET · 153

WYNFORD RD. · MURIEL · Canal Tunnel · TOLPUDDLE · 30 73

CALSHOT · RODNEY · RISINGHILL ST. · CHAPEL · BARON · ION ST.

Pentonville

COLLIER · STREET · DONEGAL · ST. · WHITE · Crafts Council & Gallery

CALEDONIAN · A5203 · Canal · 359

STREET · ROAD · 2

PENTONVILLE · A501 · 30 73 214 · CLAREMONT SQUARE · MYDDELTON · '83

KING'S · WESTON RISE · PENTON RISE · AMWELL · INGLEBERT ST. · RIVER ST. · SQUARE

CROSS · ST. · H

BRITANNIA ST. · Royal National Throat, Nose & Ear Hospital · PERCY · GT. · PERCY · ST. · LLOYD · 3

SWINTON ST. · Royal scot · PERCY CIRCUS · RIVER ST.

ACTON · ST. · Clerkenwell Magistrates Court · LLOYD SQUARE · Thames Water Authority Head Office

GRAY'S · FREDERICK · CUBITT · WHARTON · ST. · HARDWICK ST. · Finsbury Town H. · 4

London Ryan · LLOYD BAKER ST. · 17 45 46 · 63 221 259 359 · STREET · MARGERY · ST. · TYSOE ST.

INN · A5200 · PAKENHAM · Mount Pleasant · FARRINGDON · EXMOUTH MARKET · **Clerkenwell**

Kingsway nceton Coll. · H · Eastman Dental Hospital · PHOENIX · Post Office Mount Pleasant · AV. · 5 · BOWLING

MECKLENBURGH SQ. · CALTHORPE · GOUGH · 63 221 59 · GRN.

Mecklenburgh Sq. Gdns. · DOUGHTY · ROSEBERY · ROAD · 171A · FARR

D · BURGH · MILLMAN · E · 63 · Dickens House · F · WARNER ST. · TILL RAY ST.

DOUGHTY M. · ROGER · ST. · 531 · I.T.N.

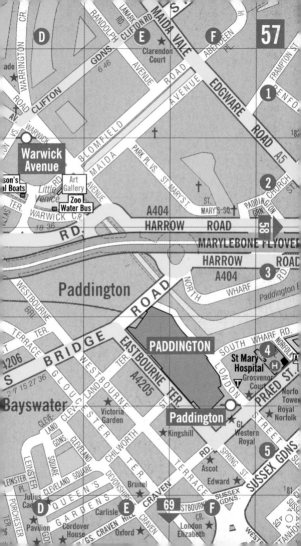

D

WARRINGTON CR.

RANDOLPH

LANARK RD.

CLIFTON RD.

E

CLIFTON GDNS 6 46

Clarendon Court

MAIDA VALE

ABERDEEN PL.

F

FRAMPTON ST.

1

PENFO

WARRINGTON

CLIFTON

ROAD AV.

CLIFTON

WARWICK

BLOMFIELD

AVENUE

ROAD

MAIDA

AVENUE

PARK PL VS.

ST. MARY'S ST.

EDGWARE ROAD A5

182

Warwick Avenue

son's
al Boats

Little Venice

WATER

Art Gallery

Zoo
Water Bus

ROAD

WARWICK CR.

18 36

RD.

2

ST. MARY'S SQ.

PADDINGTON GRN

CHURCH ST.

A404

HARROW ROAD

58

MARYLEBONE FLYOVER

WESTBOURNE

BBV

TER.

HARROW ROAD

A404

NORTH

WHARF

Paddington B

3

RD.

Paddington

BRIDGE

ROAD

EASTBOURNE TER.

A4205

WESTBOURNE

LAND

TERRACE

PADDINGTON

SOUTH WHARF RD.

St Mary's Hospital

Grosvenor Court

H

NORBOL

4

A

Norfo
Towe
Royal
Norfolk

4206

WESTBOURNE

TER.

GLOUCESTER

CLEVE-
LAND
GDNS.

CLEVELAND SQUARE

Bayswater

CRAVEN

Victoria Garden

CHILWORTH

DEVONSHIRE

LONDON

ST.

Kingshill

Paddington

Gt
Western
Royal

PRAED ST.

STREET

ROYAL

5

SUSSEX GDNS.

LEINSTER PL.

QUEEN'S

TER.

Brunel

RD.

Ascot

SPRING ST.

181

GARDENS

CLEVELAND

TERRACE

Edward

SUSSEX
GDNS.

WEST

Julius Cae

Pavilion

Cordover House

D

Carlisle

CRAVEN HILL

E

Oxford

CRAVEN

STBOURN
CR.

69

F

London Elizabeth

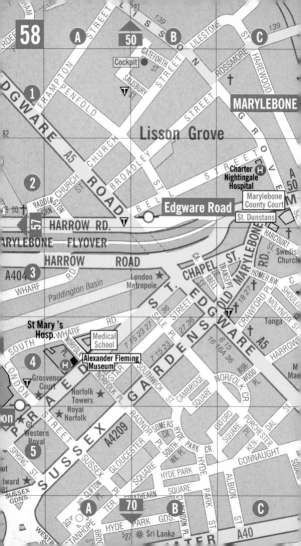

58

A STREET **50** **B** LILESTONE **C** 139

139 527

EDGWARE A5

1

FRAMPTON

PENFOLD

Cockpit ●

GATEFORTH ST.

SALISBURY ST. ▽

CHURCH

ROAD

BRADLEY

2

PADDINGTON GRN.

CHURCH ST.

82

57 HARROW RD. ▽

Lisson Grove

BELL

LISSON

STREET

STREET

ROSSMORE

HAREWOOD

MARYLEBONE

STREET

GROVE

Charter
Nightingale
Hospital **H**

Marylebone
County Court

Edgware Road ○ St. Dunstans

50 **A**
M

HARCOURT

ARYLEBONE — FLYOVER

HARROW   ROAD

A404 **3**

WHARF

Paddington Basin

London ★
Metropole

ST. Swedis
Church

CHAPEL ST.

BELL

TRANSP.

MARYLEBONE

ST.

SALE

STREET

PL.

EDGWARE

OLD

RD.

HOMER RW. C

18 27

CRAWFORD PL.

Tonga

★

MOLYNEUX ST.

SHOULD

St Mary's
Hosp.

SOUTH

WHARF RD.

Medical
School

Alexander Fleming
Museum

4

Grosvenor
Court ▽

★

LONDON

Norfolk
Towers ★

Royal
Norfolk

7 15 23 27

NORFOLK

SOUTHWICK

PL.

7 15 23

16 6A 36

6 15

NORFOLK

CAMBRIDGE

SQUARE

A5

HARROW

NORFOLK CR.

WOOD

PL.

M

M

PRAED

STREET

Gt
Western
Royal

★

5

SPRING ST.

ot

dward

SUSSEX
GDNS.

SUSSEX

CLIFTON

A4209

SUSSEX

GLOUCESTER

RADNOR

SOMERS CR.

SOUTH-
WK PL.

HYDE PARK CR.

HYDE

OXFORD

SQUARE

PORCHESTER

KEN-

DAL

CONNAUGHT

A TER.

70

ON

STANHOPE

HYDE PARK GDS.

SQUARE

HYDE PARK

HEATHERN

B

CADOGAN PL.

PARK

ALBION

C

A40

527 ★ Sri Lanka

GARDENS

GLOUCESTER

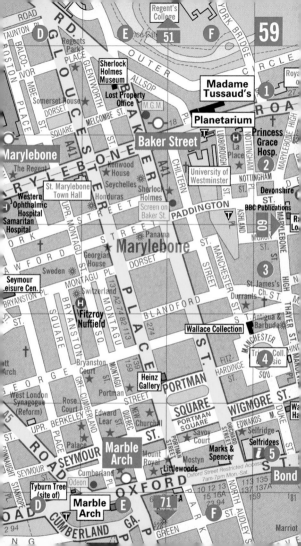

60 A **52** **Diorama Arts Centre** B C **Great Portland Street**

CIRCLE OUTER York GA. GE. UPR. HARLEY PARK SQ. WEST ST. PARK EAST OSN OSMBURG ST.

RD. PARK C.R. GREENWELL ST.

Madame Tussaud's 1

Royal Academy of Music 27 A2 30

Regent's Park

Royal National Orthopaedic Hosp.

H

MARYLEBONE ROAD

Planetarium

London Clinic

Institute for the Blind

BOLSOVER ST.

Princess Grace Hosp. La Place H NOTTINGHAM

LUXBOROUGH MARYLEBONE HIGH DEVONSHIRE ST. Chile

Portland Hosp.

CARBURT ST. GREAT PORTLAND ST. CLI

sity of ster 2 TINGHAM DEVONSHIRE BEAU MONT ST.

Devonshire H **King Edward VII Hosp. for Officers**

Poland Kenya Sierra Leone Langham Court China

Central Orthodox Synagogue

BBC Publications C2 135

TON **Radio London** MARYLEBONE WEYMOUTH ST.

Clinic

Broadcasting House

MANCHESTER ST. MOXON ST. WESTMORELAND ST. MPOLE A4201 PL. LANGHAM

3 NEW CAVENDISH ST. All Souls LANGHAM

St. James's Ch. ST. **Clifton Ford** WELBECK QUEEN ANNE ST. Namibia RIDI

Durrants HIGH THAYER ST. **Queen's College** CHANDOS ST. **Langham Hilton**

Antigua & Barbuda Hinde St. Meth Ch. ST. **CAVENDISH PLACE**

Collection MANCHESTER HINDE BENTINCK ST. **Wigmore Hall**

4 **Trinity Coll. of Music** SQU. MANDEVILLE St. Londoner **University**

FITZ- HARDING ST. Mandeville A5204 **STREET** Slovenia Belize MARGAR

QUEEN CAVENDISH SQUARE

College of Nursing

PRINCE'S ST. HOLLES ST.

British Home Stores

WIGMORE STREET HENRIETTA PL. **John Lewis**

EDWARDS M. DUKE ST. **D.H. Evans** Regent Ha

Waldegrave Hall **British Music Centre** VERE OLD CAVENDISH ST.

ORCHARD **Selfridge** JAMES ST. **Debenhams** HARE- WOOD

Marks & Spencer 5 **Selfridges** Botswana Berkshire ST. **OXFORD** ST. **Woolworth** HANOVER PRINCE

Oxford Street Restricted Access 7am-7pm Mon.-Sat. A40 **West One** **Bond St.** **Phillips Auctioneers** NEW BOND ST. SQUARE ST. GEORGE ST.

12 13 113 135 2 16A 137 137A 3 94 159 NORTH AUDLEY ST. DAVIES ST. A **72** B DUKE ST. BROOK ST. **Claridges** C MADDOX

Marriot Canada

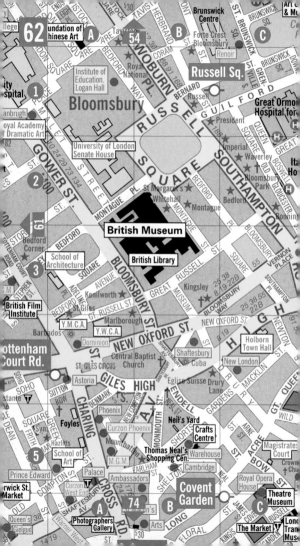

A Foundation of Chinese Art

54

B Brunswick Centre

Forte Crest Bloomsbury

C St. BRUNSWICK SQ.

Renoir

Royal National

Russell Sq.

Institute of Education. Logan Hall

Bloomsbury

Great Ormo Hospital for

ity Spital **1**

nbrugh

oyal Academy Dramatic Art

82

University of London Senate House

President

Imperial

Waverley

Old Bloomsbury Park

Ita Ho

2 GOWER ST. .00

STOP **191**

Bedford Corner

School of Architecture

BEDFORD

St Margaret's Whitehall

Montague

Bedford

Bonnin

British Museum

3

Kenilworth

British Film Institute

British Library

Kingsley

VERNON PLACE

BLOOMSBURY WAY

25 38 8 19 22B

25 38 55

St. Giles

Marlborough

GT. RUSSELL ST.

25 38 55 22B

Y.M.C.A.

Y.W.C.A.

Barbados

Dominion

NEW OXFORD ST.

Holborn Town Hall

ttenham Court Rd.

SOHO

Central Baptist Church

Shaftesbury

Cuba

New London

Astoria

Eglise Suisse

Drury Lane

GILES HIGH

stante

Foyles

Phoenix

Neil's Yard

Curzon Phoenix

Crafts Centre

5

School of Art

Mountbatten

M.G.M.

Thomas Neal's Shopping Cen.

Warehouse

Cambridge

Prince Edward

Palace

Ambassadors

Curzon West End

Covent Garden

Royal Opera House

Theatre Museum

rwick St. Market

Queen's

Gielgud

74

Photographers Gallery

Arts

The Market

Lon Tran Mus

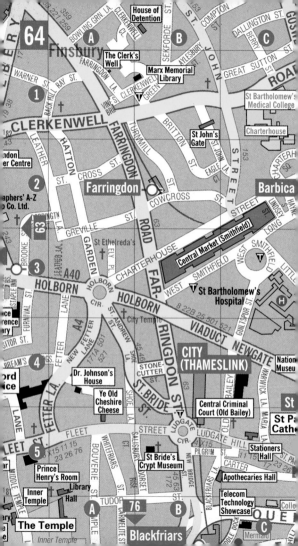

Finsbury

A   B   C

House of Detention

The Clerk's Well

Marx Memorial Library

BOWLING GRN. LA.
CLERKENWELL CL.
SEKFORDE ST.
CLERKENWELL
COMPTON ST.
DALLINGTON ST.
BERRY ST.
GT. SUTTON ST.

WARNER ST.
BACK HILL
RAY ST.
FARRINGDON LA.
VINE BRIDGE
CLERKENWELL GREEN
AYLESBURY ST.
GREAT SUTTON ST.

St Bartholomew's Medical College

Charterhouse

CLERKENWELL
LEATHER
HATTON
FARRINGDON
TURNMILL ST.
BRITTON ST.
ST. JOHN'S LA.
EAGLE CT.
ST. JOHN ST.
CHARTERH. SQ.

St John's Gate

Farringdon

CROSS ST.
GREVILLE ST.
COWCROSS ST.
SMITHFIELD ST.

Barbica

St Etheldreda's

GARDEN
LEATHER LA.
ELY PL.
BROOKE ST.
CHARTERHOUSE
FAR-
RINGDON
WEST SMITHFIELD
LONG LA.
HAYNE ST.
LINDSEY ST.
LITTL.

Central Market (Smithfield)

HOLBORN
A40
HOLBORN CIR.
HOLBORN
ST. ANDREW ST.
VIADUCT

St Bartholomew's Hospital

H

City Temple

8 22B 25 501 521

FURNIVAL ST.
FETTER LA.
NEW FETTER LANE
SHOE LANE
STONE-CUTTER ST.
ST. BRIDE ST.
BAILEY
NEWGATE

CITY (THAMESLINK)

Dr. Johnson's House

Ye Old Cheshire Cheese

Central Criminal Court (Old Bailey)

Nation Museu

WARWICK LA.
AVE MARIA LA.
OLD BAILEY

St Pa Cath

St

FLEET
FLEET ST.
BOUVERIE ST.
WHITEFRIARS ST.
SALISBURY CT.
DORSET RISE
LUDGATE CIR.
LUDGATE HILL
PILGRIM ST.
CARTER LA.

4 X15 11 15 23 26 76

4X15 11 23 26

St Bride's Crypt Museum

Stationers Hall

Prince Henry's Room

Library

Inner Temple Hall

Apothecaries Hall

Telecom Technology Showcase

Colle

The Temple

Inner Temple

A   TUDOR ST.   **76**   B

CARMELITE ST.
BLACKFRIARS
TEMPLE AV.
NEW BRIDGE ST.

Blackfriars

QUE

Mermaid

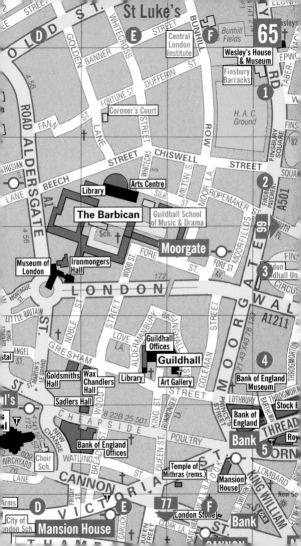

St Luke's

65

OLD ST.
D
STREET
GOLDEN
WHITECROSS
STREET
BUNHILL

E
Central
London
Institute
F
Bunhill
Fields

Wesley's House
& Museum

WESLEYS
EPWO

TABER-

BANNER
DUFFERIN ST.

Finsbury
Barracks

1

FORTUNE ST.

H. A. C.
Ground

FINS

FINSBURY
SQUARE

FAN

ROAD ALDERSGATE

4 56

Coroner's Court

STREET
WHITEC'RS
CHISWELL
STREET
STREET

FINS

SQUA

HUSIAN
S
LANE
BEECH
STREET

A1

SILK
MILTON LA.
MOOR LA.
ROPEMAKER
STREET

2
FINS'
PAVEMEN
A501
SOUTH
PL

4 56

Library
Arts Centre

The Barbican

Sch. †

Guildhall School
of Music & Drama

Moorgate

99

FIN

Museum of
London
Ironmongers
Hall

WOOD ST.
FORE
ST.

FORE
ST.
KV.

MOORFIELDS

3
don
dhall Un
CIRCUS

MORTAGUE
ST.

L O N D O N

172

MOORGATE

WALL
A1211

LITTLE BRITAIN
KING
ST.

NOBLE STREET

GRESHAM STREET

LOVE LA.

BASINGHALL STREET

Guildhall
Offices

Guildhall

ALDERMANBURY

COLEMAN STREET

THROGMORTON

BARTH'M

ANGEL
ST.
tal

Goldsmiths
Hall
Wax
Chandlers
Hall

Library

Art Gallery

2 43 X43 76 133

Bank of England
Museum

4

l's
ST. MARTIN'S LE GRAND

Sadlers Hall

WOOD ST.

B 22B 25 501

KING ST.

PRINCE'S STREET

LOTHBURY

Bank of
England

Stock Ex

THREAD

4 741 502
609

CHEAPSIDE

BREAD ST.

QUEEN ST.

POULTRY

BARTHM

Bank

Roy

5

N
NEW
CHANGE
772

Choir
Sch.

Bank of England
Offices

WATLING

Temple of
Mithras (rems.)

Mansion
House

LOMBARD

ORN

KING WILLIAM

S
609
HURCHYARD

LANE

FRIDAY ST.

BOW LA.
WALBROOK

ST. SWITHIN'S LA.

Arms

City of
ndon Sch.

D

Mansion House

VICTORIA ST.
GARLICK

E

77

QUEEN ST.

CLOAK LA.

London Stone
F
ST.

Bank

T

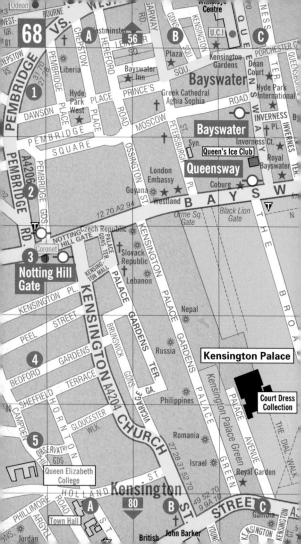

SQUARE

LEINSTER PL.

GLOUCESTER

CHESTER

TERRACE

ROAD

Ascot

RING ST.

ard

18

D CLEVELAND SQUARE E 57 F SUSSEX GDNS.

LEINSTER

Julius Caesar

QUEEN'S

DEVONSHIRE

WESTBOURNE

S

PORCHESTER

GARDENS

Pavilion

Carlisle

CRAVEN HILL

CRAVEN

CR.

London

Elizabeth

WEST

BOURNE

STREET

1

Cordover House

Oxford

Mornington Lancaster

STANHOPE

Blakemore

CRAVEN HL. GS.

Plaza on Hyde Park

Henry VIII

London Toy & Model Mus.

GATE

York

Hong Kong Student Cen.

Charles Dickens

Commadore

LANCASTER

Lancaster

SUSS

● **Lancaster Gat**

Queen's Park

LEINSTER TER.

Whites

Marlborough Gate

2

Latvia

Park Court

The Fountains

ntral

Hospital

Lancaster Gate

WALK

B U C

TER

Porchester Ter. Gate

WALK

THE

70

Gate

Lancaster Gate

LANCASTER

LONG

Speke's Monument

WALK

3

BUDGE'S

Peter Pan Statue

WATER

K E N S I N G T O N

4

ROUND POND

Serpentine Gallery

G A R D E N S

WALK

WALK

5

FLOWER

WALK

WALK

Albert Memorial

SOUTH

D THE E Queen's 81 F Alexandra Hampste

Palace Gate

Gate

Gate

Kensington Palace

Albert

Royal College of Art

K E N S N G T O N R

Royal Geographical

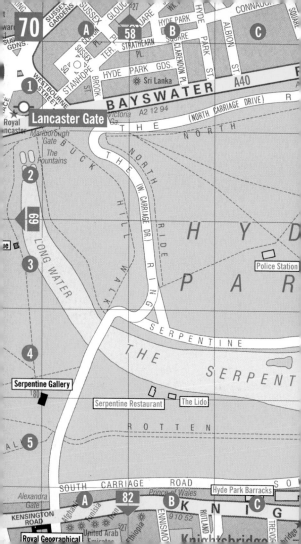

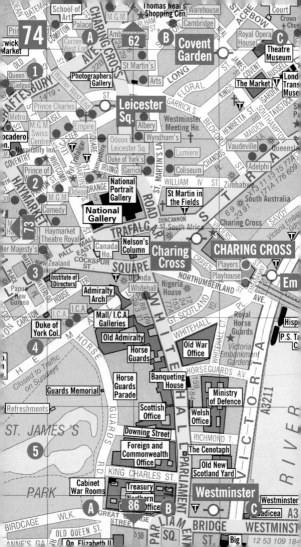

74

School of Art

CHARING CROSS

M.G.M.

Thomas Neal's Shopping Cen.

Warehouse

ST.

ACRE

BOW

Court Crown Ch

Palace

Curzon West End

Ambers

62

St Martin's

Cambridge

Royal Opera House

Covent Garden

C

Theatre Museum

Prin

wick Market

OLD

A

B

Queen's Gielgud

SHAFTESBURY

Photographers Gallery

Warner West End

14/19

ST.

Arts

LONG

FLORAL

BEDFORD

KING

COVENT

HENRIETTA

JAMES

TAVISTOCK

MAIDEN

The Market

Lond Trans Mus

1

Prince Charles

ISLE

Metro

M.G.M.

Swiss Centre

Empire

GARRICK S.

Westminster Meeting Ho.

Queensb

Leicester Sq.

Albery

Lumiere

Vaudeville

Adelphi

cadero n.

Hospitality Inn

Odeon Leicester Sq.

Wyndham's

Duke of York's

MARTIN'S

COVENTRY

Prince of

ORANGE

WHITCOMB

Garrick

Coliseum

CHANDOS

STRAND

Zimbabwe

2

M.G.M.

Odeon

National Portrait Gallery

WILLIAM IV ST

AY13 11 13 15 77A

171A 176 609

Comedy

St Martin in the Fields

73

HAYMARKET

Haymarket Theatre Royal

National Gallery

TRAFALGAR

DUNCANNON

South Africa

69 23 91

South Australia

Charing Cross

SAVOY

r Majesty's

PALL

MALL

EAST

Nelson's Column

Charing Cross

CHARING CROSS

Victoria Emba Gov

New Zealand

COCKSPUR

Canada Ho.

SQUARE

Players

CRAVEN

Em

3

Institute of Directors

Uganda

Whitehall

NORTHUMBERLAND

Playhouse

Papua New Guinea

CARLTON

I.C.A.

Admiralty Arch

Nigeria House

GT. SCOTLAND

Hisp

P.S. Ta

Duke of York Col.

Mall/ I.C.A. Galleries

Old Admiralty

WHITEHALL

Royal Horse Guards

4

HORSE

Horse Guards

Old War Office

Victoria Embankment Gardens

Closed to Traffic on Sundays

Guards Memorial

GUARDS

Horse Guards Parade

HORSEGUARDS AV.

A3211

RIVER

Banqueting House

Scottish Office

Ministry of Defence

Welsh Office

ST. JAMES'S

5

Downing Street

RICHMOND T.

Foreign and Commonwealth Office

The Cenotaph

VICTORIA

Old New Scotland Yard

PARK

KING CHARLES ST.

Refreshments

BIRDCAGE

Cabinet War Rooms

A

GREAT

Treasury Northern Office

86

B

PARLIAMENT

Westminster

C

Westminster adicea

A3

ANNE'S GA

Qn. Elizabeth II

OLD QUEEN ST.

STREET

SQ.

BRIDGE

ST.

Big

WESTMINST

12 53 109 18

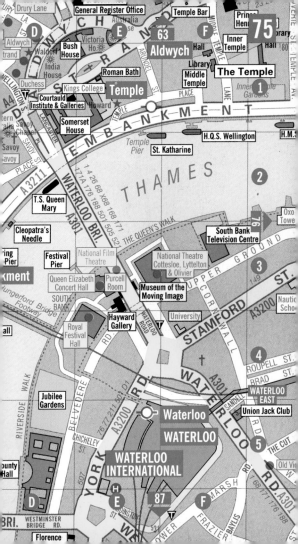

Prince
ry's Room
Library
Hall

St Bride's
Crypt Museum

CARTER

Hall

Apothecaries Hall

A

64

B

Telecom
Technology
Showcase

C

QUE

Colle

Temple

TUDOR

CARMELITE ST.

Blackfriars

Mermaid

U P P E

The Temple

TEMPLE AV.

1

Inner Temple
Gardens

PUDDLE DOCK

WHITE

LION

BLACKFRIARS

BLACKFRIARS
UNDERPASS

VICTORIA   EMBKT.

H.Q.S. Wellington

H.M.S. President

BLACKFRIARS BRI.

A201

R I V E R

2

45 63
172

Oxo
Tower

GROUND

Bankside
Gallery

THE QUEE

Bankside
Station (
(Prop. site
Tate Lo

75

South Bank
Television Centre

BLACKFRIARS

ST.

SOUTHWARK

HOPTON

HOLLAND

SUMN

3

Nautical
School

149

STAMFORD

A3200

CORNWALL

HATFE

**Sports
Centre**

BURREL

BEAR

ST.

LA.

SUFFOLK

LAVING

MEYMOTT

ST.

A201

Southwar

4

ROUPELL

ST.

BRAD

UNION

GREAT

COPPER

A301

**WATERLOO
EAST**

CUT

Stationer

SANDELL

WATERLOO

THE

Union Jack Club

Young Vic

Southwark
College

SURREY

ROW

STR

SUFFC

OO

ROAD

5

Old Vic

BUFFORD

ST.

POCOCK

45 63
172

MARSH

ROAD

WEBBE

ARD.

A

88

R

B

STREET

C

FRAZIER

WEBBER RW.

Teacher
Training

LANCAS

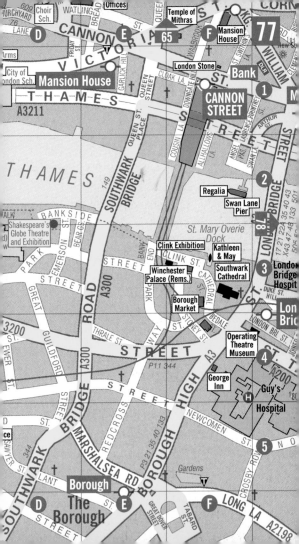

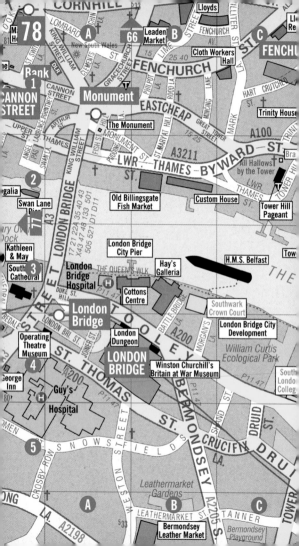

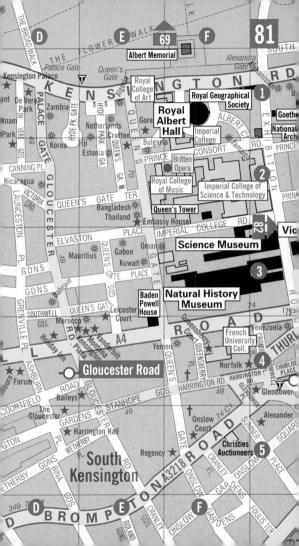

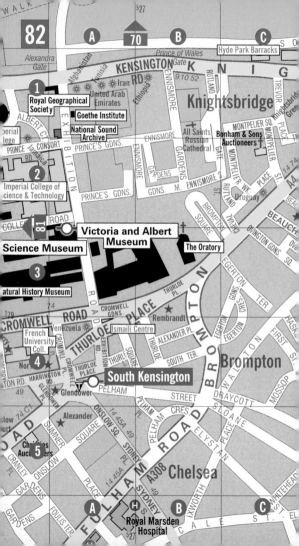

WALK

527

Alexandra Gate

Prince of Wales Gate

Hyde Park Barracks

KENSINGTON RD

9 10 52

K N I G

Afghanistan
Tunisia
*Iran

Ethiopia
RUTLAND

TREVOR

United Arab
Emirates

ENNISMORE

Knightsbridge

Knightsbridge Green

Ⓐ **Royal Geographical
Society**

■ **Goethe Institute**

■ **National Sound
Archive**

All Saints
Russian
Cathedral

MONTPELIER SQ.

MONTPELIER

PLACE

ST.

perial
ollege

ALBERT CT.

PRINCE Jamaica
CONSORT RD.

PRINCE'S GDNS.

**Bonham & Sons
Auctioneers**

MONTPELIER WK

Uruguay

PLACE

A4

ENNISMORE

ENNISMORE

GARDENS

RUTLAND

74 74

Ⓑ

**Imperial College of
Science & Technology**

PRINCE'S GDNS.

GDNS. M.

ENNISMORE S.

ST.

BEA

COLLE

81

ROAD

**Victoria and Albert
Museum**

†

BROMPTON

SQUARE

BEAUCH

OVINGTON GDNS.

OV

Science Museum

The Oratory

EGERTON TER.

OVINGTON

SQ.

Ⓒ **Natural History Museum**

74

CROMWELL GDNS

THURLOE PL.

EGERTON GDNS CRES.

EGERTON GDNS

FIRST

FASH

170

CROMWELL ROAD

★ Rembrandt

EGERTON

ST.

CROMWELL

**French
University
Coll.**

Venezuela

THURLOE

PLACE

★ Ismaili Centre

ALEXANDER PL.

EGERTON

EGERTON

TER.

★

Nor

Ⓓ

CROMWELL PL.

EXHIBITION

THURLOE

THURLOE

SQUARE

SOUTH TER.

WALTON

Brompton

MOSSOP

TON RD. HARRINGTON RD.

THURLOE
PLACE

South Kensington

PELHAM

STREET

DRAYCOTT

GLENDOWER PL.

49

▼ Glendower

PELHAM CRES.

SLOANE

ELYSTAN

low 74 CT.
urt

★ Alexander

ONSLOW SQ.

SUMNER PL.

SYDNEY PL.

PELHAM PL.

ROAD

WHITEHEA

Ⓔ **Christies
Auctioneers**

ONSLOW

SQUARE

PLACE

74 45A

SYDNEY

A308

49

Chelsea

CRANLEY
GARDENS

ONSLOW

14 45A PL.

IXWORTH

GALE

ST.

FOULIS TER.

F U L H A M

PLACE

SYDNEY

B

IXWORTH

C

EL

GARDENS

Ⓐ

H **Royal Marsden
Hospital**

Ⓑ

Ⓒ

84

Hyde Park Corner

Wellington Monument

CONSTITUTION
Closed to Traffic on Sundays

A **72** **B** **C**

Wellington Arch

BUCKINGHAM PALACE GARDENS

GROSVENOR CR.

keley

Luxembourg

CRES **1**

HALKIN ST.

Mexico

Syria

gal

GROSVENOR

CHAPEL

Turkey

Malaysia

BELGRAVE

Republic of Ireland

Trinidad & Tobago

Ivory Coast

Buckingham Palace

Queen
Galle

A12 8 16 25 38 52 73 82

A302 PLACE

The Royal Mews

2

Brunei

stria

Germany

Lesotho

HESH

LACE

UPPER BELGRAVE ST.

Saudi Arabia

Norway

WILTON

Bolivia

Finland

Belgium

BELGRAVE PLACE

Hungary

PLACE

SQUARE

HOBART

CHESTER

ST.

EATON

LWR. GROSVENOR PL.
Royal Westminster

GROSVENOR GDNS.

GROSVENOR GDNS.

GROSVENOR BR.

ROAD

Goring

ALLINGT

London Visitor & Convention Bureau

Victoria Pa

3

The
Diplomat

EATON

LYALL

SQUARE

A3217

SQU.

EATON

LWR BELGRAVE

EBURY

SQUARE

ECCLESTON

BELGRAVE

Grosvenor Thistle

ERMINUS

PALACE

Grosvenor

Ebury
Court

211 239
11 C1 C10

VICTORIA

Victoria Place Shopping Centre

4

79

eland

of

EDEN
PL.

EATON

EATON PL.

CHESTER

ELIZABETH

NC

SOUTH EATON

ROW

Colin
Ho.

Chesham Ho.

Lewis
Ho.

Pyms

† Belgravia

C1

ECCLESTON

EBURY

ST.

A1

ECCLESTON

A3214

ECCLESTON

STREET

BRI.

Scandic
Crown

BRIDGE

B

Sloane Square

WHITT-
AKER
ST.

CHESTER

TERY

ROW

SEMLEY

EBURY

GUNDY
ST.

Chester Ho.

Victoria Coach Station **T**

Grosvenor Hall

BUCKINGHAM

ELIZABETH

HUGH

ST.

C1

PALACE BRI.

Eccleston Cha
H.

SQUARE

5

BOURN

Carmel Hall

STREET

EBURY

BRI. RD.

EBURY BRI.

ALDERNEY

Elizabeth

WARW

ALDERNEY ST.

Airway

211 239

PIMLICO **ROAD** **†** **A** **B** **C**

BARNABAS

ST.

Windermere

Chelsea Barracks

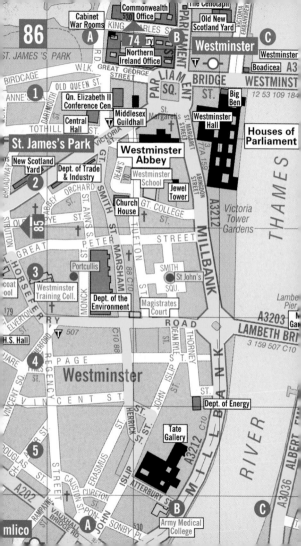

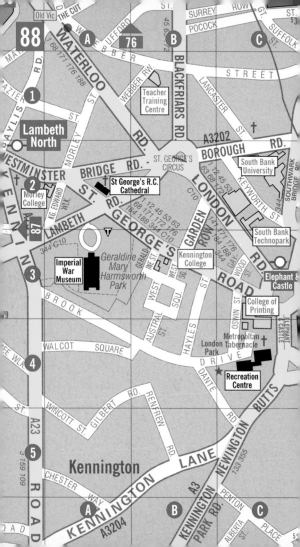

INDEX TO STREETS

Abbreviations:

All : Alley
App : Approach
Arc : Arcade
Av : Avenue
Bk : Back
Boulevd : Boulevard
Bri : Bridge
B'way : Broadway
Bldgs : Buildings
Bus : Business
Cen : Centre
Chu : Church
Chyd : Churchyard
Circ : Circle
Cir : Circus
Clo : Close
Comn : Common
Cotts : Cottages
Ct : Court
Cres : Crescent
Dri : Drive
E : East
Embkmt : Embankment
Est : Estate
Gdns : Gardens
Ga : Gate
Gt : Great
Grn : Green
Gro : Grove

Ho : House
Ind : Industrial
Junct : Junction
La : Lane
Lit : Little
Lwr : Lower
Mnr : Manor
Mans : Mansions
Mkt : Market
M : Mews
Mt : Mount
N : North
Pal : Palace
Pde : Parade
Pk : Park
Pas : Passage
Pl : Place
Rd : Road
S : South
Sq : Square
Sta : Station
St : Street
Ter : Terrace
Up : Upper
Vs : Villas
Wlk : Walk
W : West
Yd : Yard

Broadgate Sq. EC2 —2B 66
Broadley St. NW8 —2A 58
Broad Wlk. W1 —3E 71
Broad Wlk., The. W8 —3C 68
Broadway. SW1 —2F 85
Broadwick St. W1 —5E 61
Brompton Rd. SW3 —4B 82
Brompton Sq. SW7 —2B 82
Brook Dri. SE11 —3A 88
Brooke St. EC1 —3F 63
Brook Ga. W1 —2E 71
Brook St. W1 —1A 72
Brook St. W2 —1A 70
Brownlow St. WC1 —3E 63
Brunswick Gdns. W8 —4A 68
Brunswick Sq. WC1 —5C 54
Brush Field St. E1 —2B 66
Bruton St. W1 —2C 72
Bryanston Pl. W1 —3D 59
Bryanston Sq. W1 —3D 59
Buck Hill Wlk. W2 —2A 70
Buckingham Ga. SW1 —1D 85
Buckingham Pal. Rd. SW1
                          —5B 84
Budge's Wlk. W2 —3E 69
Bunhill Row. EC1 —1F 65
Burlington Arc. W1 —2D 73
Burlington Gdns. W1 —2D 73
Burrell St. SE1 —3B 76
Burwood Pl. W2 —4C 58
Buxton St. E1 —1E 67
Byward St. EC3 —2B 78

Cabbell St. NW1 —3B 58
Cable St. E1 —1F 79
Cadogan Gdns. SW3 —4E 83
Cadogan La. SW1 —3F 83
Cadogan Pl. SW1 —2E 83
Cadogan Sq. SW1 —3D 83
Cadogan St. SW3 —5D 83
Caledonian Rd. N1 —2C 54
Caledonia St. N1 —2C 54
Cale St. SW3 —5B 82
Calshot St. N1 —1D 55
Calthorpe St. WC1 —5E 55
Cambridge Sq. W2 —4B 58
Camden High St. NW1 —1D 53
Camden St. NW1 —1E 53
Camley St. NW1 —1A 54
Camomile St. EC3 —4B 66
Campden Hill Rd. W8 —4A 68
Candover St. W1 —3D 61
Canning Pl. W8 —2D 81
Cannon St. EC4 —5D 65
Carburton St. W1 —2C 60
Cardington St. NW1 —3E 53

Carey St. WC2 —5E 63
Carlisle La. SE1 —3E 87
Carlisle Pl. SW1 —3D 85
Carlisle St. W1 —5F 61
Carlos Pl. W1 —2B 72
Carlton Gdns. SW1 —4F 73
Carlton Ho. Ter. SW1 —4F 73
Carmelite St. EC4 —1A 76
Carnaby St. W1 —5D 61
Carnegie St. N1 —1E 55
Carter La. EC4 —5C 64
Carthusian St. EC1 —2D 65
Carting La. WC2 —2C 74
Cartwright Gdns. WC1 —4B 54
Cartwright St. E1 —1E 79
Castellain Rd. W9 —1C 56
Castle La. SW1 —2D 85
Cathedral Plazza. SW1 —3D 85
Cathedral St. SE1 —3F 77
Catton St. WC1 —3D 63
Causton St. SW1 —5A 86
Cavendish Av. NW8 —2A 50
Cavendish Clo. NW8 —3A 50
Cavendish Pl. W1 —4C 60
Cavendish Sq. W1 —4C 60
Caxton St. SW1 —2E 85
Centaur St. SE1 —2E 87
Chalton St. NW1 —1E 53
Chambers St. SE1 —5F 79
Chancery La. WC2 —3E 63
Chandos Pl. WC2 —2B 74
Chandos St. W1 —3C 60
Chapel Mkt. N1 —1F 55
Chapel St. NW1 —3B 58
Chapel St. SW1 —2A 84
Chapter St. SW1 —5F 85
Charing Cross Rd. WC2 —4A 62
Charlbert St. NW8 —1B 50
Charles II St. SW1 —3F 73
Charles St. W1 —3B 72
Charlotte St. W1 —2E 61
Charlotte Ter. N1 —1E 55
Charlwood St. SW1 —5E 85
Charrington St. NW1 —1F 53
Charterhouse Sq. EC1 —2C 64
Charterhouse St. EC1 —3A 64
Cheapside. EC2 —5D 65
Chenies Pl. NW1 —1A 54
Chenies St. WC1 —2F 61
Cheniston Gdns. W8 —2B 80
Chepstow Pl. W2 —5A 56
Chepstow Rd. W2 —4A 56
Chepstow Vs. W11 —1A 68
Chesham Pl. SW1 —3F 83
Chesham St. SW1 —3F 83
Cheshire St. E2 —1E 67
Chesterfield Gdns. W1 —3B 72

Chesterfield Hill. W1 —2B 72
Chesterfield St. W1 —3B 72
Chester Ga. NW1 —4C 52
Chester Rd. NW1 —4A 52
Chester Row. SW1 —5F 83
Chester Sq. SW1 —4A 84
Chester St. SW1 —2A 84
Chester Ter. NW1 —3B 52
Chester Way. SE11 —5A 88
Cheval Pl. SW7 —2C 82
Chicheley St. SE1 —5E 75
Chicksand St. E1 —3E 67
Chiltern St. W1 —2F 59
Chilton St. E2 —1E 67
Chilworth St. W2 —5E 57
Chippenham Rd. W9 —1A 56
Chiswell St. EC1 —2E 65
Church St. W2 & NW8 —2A 58
Churchway. NW1 —3A 54
Churton St. SW1 —5E 85
Circus Rd. NW8 —3A 50
City Rd. EC1 —1A 66
Claremont Sq. N1 —2F 55
Clarendon Pl. W2 —1B 70
Clarendon St. SW1 —5C 84
Clements La. EC4 —1A 78
Clerkenwell Grn. EC1 —1A 64
Clerkenwell Rd. EC1 —1F 63
Cleveland Gdns. W2 —5D 57
Cleveland Row. SW1 —4E 73
Cleveland Sq. W2 —5D 57
Cleveland St. W1 —1C 60
Cleveland Ter. W2 —5D 57
Clifford St. W1 —2D 73
Clifton Gdns. W9 —1D 57
Clifton Pl. W2 —5A 58
Clifton Rd. W9 —1E 57
Clifton St. EC2 —2B 66
Clifton Vs. W9 —2D 57
Clink St. SE1 —3F 77
Clipstone St. W1 —2C 60
Cliveden Pl. SW1 —4F 83
Cloak La. EC4 —1E 77
Cloudesley Rd. N1 —1F 55
Cobourg St. NW1 —4E 53
Cockspur St. SW1 —3A 74
Colchester St. E1 —4E 67
Coleman St. EC2 —4F 65
College Pl. NW1 —1E 53
Collier St. N1 —2D 55
Collingham Gdns. SW5 —5C 80
Collingham Rd. SW5 —4C 80
Commercial Rd. E1 —4F 67
Commercial St. E1 —1D 67
Compton St. EC1 —1B 64
Conduit St. W1 —1C 72
Connaught Sq. W2 —5D 59

Connaught St. W2 —5C 58
Constitution Hill. SW1 —5B 72
Conway St. W1 —1D 61
Cooper's Row. EC3 —1D 79
Copenhagen St. N1 —1F 55
Copperfield St. SE1 —5C 76
Coram St. WC1 —1B 62
Cornhill. EC3 —5A 66
Cornwall Gdns. SW7 —3C 80
Cornwall Rd. SE1 —3F 75
Cosser St. SE1 —2F 87
Courtfield Gdns. SW5 —5C 80
Courtfield Rd. SW7 —5D 81
Cousin La. EC4 —2F 77
Covent Garden. WC2 —1C 74
Coventry St. W1 —2F 73
Cowcross St. EC1 —2B 64
Cranleigh St. NW1 —2E 53
Cranley Gdns. SW7 —5E 81
Cranley Pl. SW7 —5F 81
Craven Hill. W2 —1E 69
Craven Hill Gdns. W2 —1D 69
Craven Rd. W2 —1E 69
Craven St. WC2 —3B 74
Craven Ter. W2 —1E 69
Crawford Pl. W1 —4C 58
Crawford St. W1 —3C 58
Creechurch La. EC3 —5C 66
Crispin St. E1 —3D 67
Cristopher St. EC2 —1A 66
Cromer St. WC1 —4B 54
Cromwell Gdns. SW7 —3A 82
Cromwell Pl. SW7 —4A 82
Cromwell Rd. SW5 & SW7
—4B 80
Crosby Row. SE1 —5F 77
Crosswall. EC3 —1D 79
Crowndale Rd. NW1 —1E 53
Crucifix La. SE1 —5B 78
Crutched Friars. EC3 —1C 78
Cubitt St. WC1 —4E 55
Cumberland Ga. W2 & W1
—1D 71
Cumberland Mkt. NW1 —3C 52
Cumberland Pl. NW1 —3B 52
Cundy St. SW1 —5A 84
Cunningham Pl. NW8 —5A 50
Cureton St. SW1 —5A 86
Cursitor St. EC4 —4F 63
Curzon Ga. W1 —4A 72
Curzon St. W1 —4A 72
Cutler St. E1 —4C 66
Cut, The. SE1 —5B 76

Dallington St. EC1 —1C 64
Dante Rd. SE11 —4B 88

Dartmouth St. SW1 —1F 85
Davenant St. E1 —3F 67
Davies St. W1 —5B 60
Dawson Pl. W2 —1A 68
Deal St. E1 —2F 67
Deanery St. W1 —3A 72
Dean Ryle St. SW1 —4B 86
Dean St. W1 —5F 61
Dean's Yd. SW1 —2A 86
Delamere Ter. W2 —2C 56
Delancy St. NW1 —1B 52
Delaware Rd. W9 —1B 56
Denbigh Pl. SW1 —5D 85
Denbigh St. SW1 —5E 85
Denmark St. WC2 —4A 62
Derby St. W1 —4A 72
Derry St. W8 —1B 80
De Vere Gdns. W8 —1D 81
Devonshire Pl. W1 —1A 60
Devonshire St. W1 —2A 60
Devonshire Ter. W2 —5E 57
Dial Wlk., The. W8 —5C 68
Dock St. E1 —1F 79
Dombey St. WC1 —2D 63
Donegal St. N1 —2E 55
Doric Way. NW1 —3F 53
Dorrington St. EC1 —2F 63
Dorset Rise. EC4 —5B 64
Dorset Sq. NW1 —1D 59
Dorset St. W1 —3E 59
Doughty M. WC1 —1D 63
Doughty St. WC1 —5D 55
Douglas St. SW1 —5F 85
Dover St. W1 —2C 72
Downgate Hill. EC4 —1F 77
Downing St. SW1 —5A 74
Down St. W1 —4B 72
Doyley St. SW1 —4F 83
Drake St. WC1 —3D 63
Draycott Av. SW3 —4C 82
Draycott Pl. SW3 —5D 83
Druid St. SE1 —5C 78
Drummond Cres. NW1 —3F 53
Drummond St. NW1 —5D 53
Drury La. WC2 —4C 62
Dufferin St. EC1 —1E 65
Duke's Pl. EC3 —5C 66
Duke St. SW1 —3E 73
Duke St. W1 —5A 60
Duke St. Hill. SE1 —3A 78
Dunbridge St. E2 —1F 67
Duncannon St. WC2 —2B 74

Eagle Ct. EC1 —2B 64
Eagle St. WC1 —3D 63
Earlham St. WC2 —5B 62

Earl's Ct. Gdns. SW5 —5B 80
Earl's Ct. Rd. W8 & SW5 —2A 80
Earl's Ct. Sq. SW5 —5B 80
Eastbourne Ter. W2 —4E 57
Eastcastle St. W1 —4D 61
Eastcheap. EC3 —1B 78
E. Smithfield. E1 —2E 79
Eaton Ga. SW1 —4F 83
Eaton Pl. SW1 —3F 83
Eaton Sq. SW1 —4F 83
Eaton Ter. SW1 —4F 83
Ebury Bri. SW1 —5B 84
Ebury Bri. Rd. SW1 —5B 84
Ebury Sq. SW1 —5A 84
Ebury St. SW1 —5A 84
Eccleston Bri. SW1 —4C 84
Eccleston Pl. SW1 —4B 84
Eccleston Sq. SW1 —5C 84
Eccleston St. SW1 —3B 84
Edgware Rd. W2 —1F 57
Edinburgh Ga. SW1 —5D 71
Edwards M. W1 —5F 59
Egerton Cres. SW3 —4C 82
Egerton Gdns. SW3 —4B 82
Egerton Ter. SW3 —3C 82
Eldon Rd. W8 —3C 80
Eldon St. EC2 —3A 66
Elephant & Castle. SE1 —4C 88
Elgin Av. W9 —1A 56
Elizabeth Bri. SW1 —5B 84
Elizabeth St. SW1 —4A 84
Ellen St. E1 —5E 67
Elvaston Pl. SW7 —3D 81
Elverton St. SW1 —4F 85
Ely Pl. EC1 —3A 64
Elystan Pl. SW3 —5C 82
Elystan St. SW3 —5B 82
Embankment Pl. WC2 —3C 74
Emerson St. SE1 —3D 77
Endell St. WC2 —4B 62
Endsleigh Gdns. NW1 —5F 53
Endsleigh Pl. WC1 —5A 54
Endsleigh St. WC1 —5F 53
Ennismore Gdns. SW7 —1B 82
Ennismore Gdns. M. SW7
                      —2B 82
Ennismore St. SW7 —2B 82
Epworth St. EC2 —1A 66
Erasmus St. SW1 —5A 86
Essex Vs. W8 —1A 80
Euston Rd. NW1 —4F 53
Euston Sq. NW1 —4F 53
Euston St. NW1 —4E 53
Euston Underpass. NW1 —5D 53
Eversholt St. NW1 —1E 53
Ewer St. SE1 —4D 77
Exhibition Rd. SW7 —1A 82

94

Lwr. Belgrave St. SW1 —3B 84
Lwr. Grosvenor Pl. SW1 —2C 84
Lwr. James St. W1 —1E 73
Lwr. John St. W1 —1E 73
Lwr. Marsh. SE1 —1E 87
Lwr. Sloane St. SW1 —5F 83
Lwr. Thames St. EC3 —2A 78
Lowndes Sq. SW1 —1E 83
Lowndes St. SW1 —2F 83
Ludgate Cir. EC4 —5B 64
Ludgate Hill. EC4 —5B 64
Luke St. EC2 —1B 66
Luxborough St. W1 —2F 59
Lyall St. SW1 —3F 83

Mableden Pl. WC1 —4A 54
Macclesfield Bri. NW1 —1C 50
Macklin St. WC2 —4C 62
Maddox St. W1 —1C 72
Maida Av. W2 —2E 57
Maida Vale. W9 —1E 57
Maiden La. WC2 —1C 74
Malet St. WC1 —1F 61
Mall, The. SW1 —4A 74
Manchester Sq. W1 —4F 59
Manchester St. W1 —3F 59
Mandeville Pl. W1 —4A 60
Manningtree St. E1 —4F 67
Mansell St. E1 —5E 67
Maple St. W1 —2D 61
Marchmont St. WC1 —5B 54
Margaret St. W1 —4C 60
Margery St. WC1 —4F 55
Maria La. EC4 —5C 64
Mark La. EC3 —1C 78
Marlborough Rd. SW1 —4E 73
Marloes Rd. W8 —2B 80
Marshall St. W1 —5E 61
Marshalsea Rd. SE1 —5E 77
Marsham St. SW1 —3A 86
Marylands Rd. W9 —1A 56
Marylebone Flyover. W2 —3F 57
Marylebone High St. W1 —2A 60
Marylebone La. W1 —3A 60
Marylebone Rd. NW1 —2C 58
Mecklenburgh Pl. WC1 —5D 55
Mecklenburgh Sq. WC1 —5D 55
Medburn St. NW1 —1F 53
Melcombe St. NW1 —1E 59
Melton St. NW1 —4E 53
Mews St. E1 —3F 79
Meymott St. SE1 —4B 76
Middlesex St. E1 —3C 66
Middle Temple La. EC4 —5F 63
Midland Rd. NW1 —2A 54
Millbank. SW1 —3B 86

Millman St. WC1 —1D 63
Mill St. SE1 —5E 79
Mill St. W1 —1C 72
Milner St. SW3 —4D 83
Milton St. EC2 —2F 65
Mincing La. EC3 —1B 78
Minories. EC3 —5D 67
Molyneux St. W1 —3C 58
Monck St. SW1 —3A 86
Monmouth St. WC2 —5B 62
Montague Pl. WC1 —2A 62
Montague St. EC1 —3D 65
Montague St. WC1 —2B 62
Montagu Pl. W1 —3D 59
Montagu Sq. W1 —3E 59
Montagu St. W1 —4E 59
Montpelier Sq. SW7 —1C 82
Montpelier St. SW7 —1C 82
Montpelier Wlk. SW7 —2C 82
Monument St. EC3 —2A 78
Moore St. SW3 —4D 83
Moorfields. EC2 —3F 65
Moorgate. EC2 —4F 65
Moor La. EC2 —2F 65
Moreton Pl. SW1 —5E 85
Moreton St. SW1 —5F 85
Morgan's La. SE1 —4B 78
Morley St. SE1 —2A 88
Mornington Cres. NW1 —1D 53
Mornington Pl. NW1 —1C 52
Mornington St. NW1 —1C 52
Mornington Ter. NW1 —1C 52
Mortimer St. W1 —4C 60
Moscow Rd. W2 —1B 68
Mossop St. SW3 —4C 82
Motcomb St. SW1 —2F 83
Mt. Pleasant. WC1 —1E 63
Mount St. W1 —2F 71
Moxon St. W1 —3A 60
Muriel St. N1 —1E 55
Museum St. WC1 —3B 62
Myddleton Sq. EC1 —3F 55

Neal St. WC2 —4B 62
(in two parts)
Neathouse Pl. SW1 —4D 85
Nevern Pl. SW5 —5A 80
Nevern Rd. SW5 —5A 80
Nevern Sq. SW5 —5A 80
New Bond St. W1 —5B 60
New Bri. St. EC4 —5B 64
New Burlington St. W1 —1D 73
Newburn St. SE11 —5E 87
New Cavendish St. W1 —3A 60
New Change. EC4 —5D 65
Newcomen St. SE1 —5F 77

New Compton St. WC2 —5A 62
New Fetter La. EC4 —4A 64
Newgate St. EC1 —4C 64
Newington Butts. SE11 —5C 88
Newman St. W1 —3E 61
New North St. WC1 —2D 63
New Oxford St. WC1 —4A 62
Newport St. SE11 —5D 87
New Quebec St. W1 —5E 59
Newton St. WC2 —4C 62
Noble St. EC2 —4D 65
Noel St. W1 —5E 61
Norfolk Cres. W2 —4C 58
Norfolk Pl. W2 —4A 58
N. Wharf Rd —3F 57
N. Audley St. W1 —5F 59
N. Carriage Dri. W2 —1B 70
Northdown St. N1 —2D 55
N. Gower St. NW1 —4E 53
Northington St. WC1 —1E 63
Northumberland Av. WC2 —3B 74
North Wlk. W2 —2D 69
Norton Folgate. E1 —2C 66
Nottingham Pl. W1 —2F 59
Nottingham St. W1 —2F 59
Notting Hill Ga. W11 —3A 68

Oakington Rd. W9 —1A 56
Oakley Sq. NW1 —1E 53
Observatory Gdns. W8 —5A 68
Old Bailey. EC4 —5C 64
Old Bond St. W1 —2D 73
Old Broad St. EC2 —4A 66
Old Brompton Rd. SW5 & SW7
                        —5D 81
Old Cavendish St. W1 —4B 60
Old Compton St. W1 —1F 73
Old Gloucester St. WC1 —2C 62
Old Marylebone Rd. NW1 —3C 58
Old Montague St. E1 —3F 67
Old Paradise St. SE11 —4D 87
Old Pye St. SW1 —2F 85
Old Queen St. SW1 —1A 86
Old St. EC1 —1D 65
Onslow Gdns. SW7 —5F 81
Onslow Sq. SW7 —5F 81
Orange St. WC2 —2A 74
Orchard St. W1 —5F 59
Ordnance Hill. NW8 —1A 50
Ormonde Ter. NW1 —1D 51
Orsett Ter. W2 —4C 56
Osbert St. SW1 —5F 85
Osborn St. E1 —3E 67
Osnaburgh St. NW1 —5C 52
Osnaburgh Ter. NW1 —5C 52

Ossington St. W2 —2A 68
Ossulston St. NW1 —2A 54
Oswin St. SE11 —4C 88
Outer Circ. NW1 —3C 50
Ovington Gdns. SW3 —3C 82
Ovington Sq. SW3 —3C 82
Oxford Cir. W1 —5D 61
Oxford Sq. W2 —5C 58
Oxford St. W1 —5E 59

Paddington Grn. W2 —2F 57
Paddington St. W1 —2F 59
Page St. SW1 —4A 86
Pakenham St. WC1 —4E 55
Palace Av. W8 —4C 68
Palace Gdns. Ter. W8 —3A 68
Palace Ga. W8 —1D 81
Palace Grn. W8 —4B 68
Palace St. SW1 —2D 85
Pall Mall. SW1 —4E 73
Pall Mall E. SW1 —3A 74
Pancras Rd. NW1 —1F 53
Panton St. SW1 —2F 73
Park Cres. W1 —1B 60
Park La. W1 —1E 71
Park Pl. Vs. W2 —2E 57
Park Rd. NW8 & NW1 —3B 50
Park Sq. E. NW1 —5C 52
Park Sq. W. NW1 —1B 60
Park St. SE1 —3D 77
Park St. W1 —1F 71
Parkway. NW1 —1B 52
Parliament Sq. SW1 —1B 86
Parliament St. SW1 —5B 74
Paul St. EC2 —1A 66
Paveley St. NW8 —4C 50
Pavilion Rd. SW1 —1E 83
Peel St. W8 —4A 68
Pelham Cres. SW7 —5B 82
Pelham Pl. SW7 —4B 82
Pelham St. SW7 —4A 82
Pembridge Gdns. W2 —2A 68
Pembridge Pl. W2 —1A 68
Pembridge Rd. W11 —2A 68
Pembridge Sq. W2 —2A 68
Pembridge Vs. W11 —1A 68
Pembroke Rd. W8 —4A 80
Pembroke Sq. W8 —3A 80
Pembroke Vs. W8 —3A 80
Penfold St. NW8 & NW1 —1A 58
Penton Pl. SE17 —5C 88
Penton Rise. W1 —3E 55
Penton St. N1 —1F 55
Pentonville Rd. N1 —2D 55
Penywern Rd. SW5 —5A 80
Percy Cir. WC1 —3E 55

Rutherford St. SW1 —4F 85
Rutland St. SW7 —2C 82

Sackville St. W1 —2E 73
Sail St. SE11 —3E 87
St Albans Gro. W8 —2C 80
St Andrew St. EC4 —3A 64
St Ann's St. SW1 —2A 86
St Ann's Ter. NW8 —1A 50
St Barnabas St. SW1 —5A 84
St Botolph St. EC3 —4D 67
St Bride St. EC4 —4B 64
St Cross St. EC1 —2A 64
St Edmund's Ter. NW8 —1C 50
St George's Cir. SE1 —2B 88
St George's Dri. SW1 —5C 84
St George's Rd. SE1 —2A 88
St George St. W1 —1C 72
St Giles Cir. W1 —4A 62
St Giles High St. WC2 —4A 62
St James's Pl. SW1 —4D 73
St James's Sq. SW1 —3E 73
St James's St. SW1 —3D 73
St John La. EC1 —2B 64
St John St. EC1 —1B 64
St John's Wood High St. NW8
—2A 50
St John's Wood Rd. NW8
—4A 50
St John's Wood Ter. NW8
—1A 50
St Katharine's Way. E1 —3E 79
St Margaret St. SW1 —1B 86
St Martin's La. WC2 —2B 74
St Martin's le Grand. EC1
—4D 65
St Mary at Hill. EC3 —2B 78
St Mary Axe. EC3 —5B 66
St Mary's Sq. W2 —2F 57
St Mary's Ter. W2 —1F 57
St Pancras Way. NW1 —1F 53
St Paul's Chyd. EC4 —5C 64
St Petersburgh Pl. W2 —1B 68
St Swithin's La. EC4 —1F 77
St Thomas St. SE1 —1A 78
Sale Pl. W2 —4B 58
Salisbury Ct. EC4 —5B 64
Salisbury St. NW8 —1B 58
Sandell St. SE1 —5F 75
Sardinia St. WC2 —4D 63
Saville Row. W1 —1D 73
Savoy Pl. WC2 —2C 74
Savoy St. WC2 —2D 75
Scarsdale Pl. W8 —2B 80
Scarsdale Vs. W8 —3A 80
Sclater St. E1 —1D 67

Scrutton St. EC2 —1B 66
Sekforde St. EC1 —1B 64
Semley St. SW1 —5A 84
Senior St. W2 —2B 56
Serle St. WC2 —4E 63
Serpentine Rd. W2 —4B 70
Settles St. E1 —3F 67
Seymour Pl. W1 —2C 58
Seymour St. W2 & W1 —5D 59
Shad Thames. SE1 —4D 79
Shaftesbury Av. W1 & WC2
—2F 73
Shand St. SE1 —5C 78
Sheffield Ter. W8 —4A 68
Shelton St. WC2 —5B 62
Shepherd St. W1 —4B 72
Sherwood St. W1 —1E 73
Shirland Rd. W9 —1B 56
Shoe La. EC4 —4A 64
 (in two parts)
Shoreditch High St. E1 —1C 66
Shorter St. E1 —1E 79
Shorts Gdns. WC2 —5B 62
Shouldham St. W1 —3C 58
Shrewsbury Rd. W2 —4A 56
Sidmouth St. WC1 —4C 54
Silk St. EC2 —2E 65
Sloane Av. SW3 —5C 82
Sloane Gdns. SW1 —5F 83
Sloane Sq. SW1 —5E 83
Sloane St. SW1 —1E 83
Sloane Ter. SW1 —4F 83
Smith Sq. SW1 —3B 86
Snowsfields. SE1 —5A 78
Soho Sq. W1 —4F 61
Soho St. W1 —4F 61
Somers Cres. W2 —5B 58
S. Wharf Rd —4F 57
Southampton Pl. WC1 —3C 62
Southampton Row. WC1 —2C 62
Southampton St. WC2 —1C 74
S. Audley St. W1 —2A 72
S. Bank. SE1 —3D 75
S. Carriage Rd. SW7 & SW1 —70
S. Eaton Pl. SW1 —4A 84
South Pl. EC2 —2A 66
South St. W1 —3A 72
South Ter. SW7 —4B 82
Southwark Bri. SE1 & EC4 —2E 77
Southwark Bri. Rd. SE1 —2C 88
Southwark Bri. Rd. SE1 —5D 77
Southwark St. SE1 —3B 76
Southwell Gdns. SW7 —3D 81
Southwick Pl. W2 —5B 58
Southwick St. W2 —4B 58
Spital Sq. E1 —2C 66
Spital St. E1 —2E 67

101

102

INDEX TO EMBASSIES, LEGATIONS AND COMMONWEALTH REPRESENTATIVES

INDEX TO HOSPITALS

Cover Photo Woodmansterne/Jeremy Marks
Every possible care has been taken to ensure that the information given in this publication is accurate and whilst the publishers would be grateful to learn of any errors, they regret they cannot accept any responsibility for loss thereby caused.